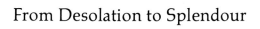

From Desolation to Splendour

From Desolation to Splendour

Changing Perceptions of the British Columbia Landscape

Maria Tippett and Douglas Cole

CLARKE, IRWIN & COMPANY LIMITED   TORONTO/VANCOUVER

Canadian Cataloguing in Publication Data.

Tippett, Maria, 1944-
   From desolation to splendour

Includes index.
ISBN 0-7720-1048-X

1. British Columbia in art. 2. Landscape in art.
3. British Columbia—Description and travel.
I. Cole, Douglas, 1938-   II. Title.

N8214.5.C2T56   709'.711   C77-001077-6

©1977 by Clarke, Irwin & Company Limited

ISBN 0-7720-1048-X

Published simultaneously in the United States
by Books Canada Inc., 33 East Tupper Street,
Buffalo, N.Y. 14203

and in the United Kingdom by Books Canada
Limited, 17 Cockspur Street, Suite 600,
London SW1Y 5BP.

1 2 3 4 5 SM 81 80 79 78 77

Printed in Canada

Contents

To
Harriet Blackie and George

What seest thou?
Cedar, pine, balsam, fir
Straight and tall, pointing always
to the blue sky, organised orderly
form. Tangles of dense undergrowth
smothering, choking, struggling,
in the distance receding plane
after plane, rising, falling—warm
and cold greens, gnarled stump
of grey and brown.

What hearest thou?
Whisperings, murmurings, now
loud, now soft, the trees talking,
squeakings, groanings, creakings,
sometimes tree trunks chafing
against each other, the saucy
screech of blue jay, the kingfisher's
clatter and the chatter of an
occasional squirrel, resenting my
intrusion.

What smellest thou?
The sweet smell of growing
things, of moist earth and sun-
ripening berries, the faint wildflower smell, the spicy smell
of new pine growth and the dear
smell of cedar when you crush it.

What feelest thou?
The reality of growth and life and
light, the sweetness of Mother
Nature, the nearness of God,
the unity of the universe,
peace, content.

What tastest thou?
—The full, pure joy of life . . .

EMILY CARR
Renfrew August 14, 1929

Preface

This book is about the landscape of British Columbia; essentially about the European's perception of it, ultimately about his discovery of its aesthetic and spiritual qualities. The terrain which Captain George Vancouver saw as desolate in 1792, F. H. Varley found heavenly in 1926. To love this land, Rupert Brooke wrote, would be "like embracing a wraith," yet Emily Carr developed a deep passion for her West.

Roy Daniells, a British Columbian, has written that "the true alpha and omega of Canadian national consciousness" is, in the last analysis, "the land, the countryside, the earth, the terrain."[1] The dominance of landscape in the consciousness and identity of Canadians and its perception by artists and writers has been abundantly documented, described and debated. This book looks only at British Columbia, a province whose landscape is both spectacular and unique; a region which presented its own peculiar problems and offered its own special qualities to those who visited or settled in it.

From Desolation to Splendour focuses upon artists who painted the British Columbia landscape. It is written with the assumption that the artist possesses a visual perception that reflects and sometimes advances that of his time. It is generally true, Lord Clark remarks, that all changes of expression of popular taste have their origins in the vision of artists "which sometimes rapidly, sometimes gradually and always unconsciously, is accepted by the uninterested man."[2] By the end of World War II both artists and the interested public had discovered and accepted the province's landscape. That process of discovery and acceptance is the theme of this book.

It is not a history of painting, even of landscape painting, in British Columbia. We have not sought to catalogue the many artists, good and bad, who have painted its scenic features. There are numerous omissions, some intentional, others imposed by the sources and pictures available to us. Our purpose is to write about the idea of landscape. This is an essay into cultural and intellectual history, not into art history.

There are many people and institutions to whom we are indebted. Grant money was seldom available for research, but at a critical juncture Dean Sam Smith of Simon Fraser University brought timely aid. The Provincial Secretary of the Province of British Columbia and the Leon and Thea Koerner Foundation generously provided funds for photography. The book has been published with the help of a grant from the Humanities Research Council of Canada, using funds provided by the Canada Council. Further assistance toward publication was provided by the Provincial Secretary of British Columbia and the Vice-President Academic, Simon Fraser University.

We are indebted to a dozen art galleries and libraries across the country and abroad. In particular we would like to express gratitude to Evelyn McMann of the Vancouver Public Library, Colin Graham of the Art Gallery of Greater Victoria, Sheila Kincaid, then of the Burnaby Art Gallery, Dennis Reid and Charles C. Hill of the National Gallery of Canada, Robert McMichael of the McMichael Canadian Conservation Collection and the staffs of those institutions and of the Vancouver Art Gallery, the Vancouver City Archives and the Centennial Museum, the Archives of British Columbia, the Seattle Art Museum, the Glenbow-Alberta Institute, the Royal Ontario Museum, the Montreal Museum of Fine Art, the Art Gallery of Ontario and the Public Archives of Canada. Artists, their relatives and friends, gave frequent and indispensable assistance. Students at Simon Fraser University provided both stimulation and information. David Barnhill lent photographic assistance. Jack Hardman and William Sampson made cogent comments on portions of the text, Evelyn McMann upon it all. Among scholars, Bernard Smiths's work in art history was an inspiration. J. Russell Harper's books were extremely useful and Wiley Thom's research into Vancouver's early art proved invaluable. We are particularly indebted to Jack Shadbolt for his Foreword and to Tod Greenaway for much of the photography.

Mayne Island, British Columbia

Foreword

Since art is more a matter of reflecting on experience than merely recording it, it is evident from the record of British Columbia chronicled in this book, as elsewhere, that only when the living pattern had established itself did the more deeply subjective responses to life on the "frontier" begin to manifest themselves. The human being inside the settler now begins to identify with his new home and in consequence his art is relieved of its practical documentary urgencies and can focus on the poetry of experience. And in British Columbia this experience is strongly identified with the landscape which by its pervasive presence dominates the imagination.

However, within the area of landscape painting we can find reflected as many kinds of personal experience and attitude as in any other area of painting. As he perceives and adjusts to the natural or external landscape the artist screens it for those attributes which are most consonant with his inner image of his relation to his environment—his internal conception of the surroundings with which he feels most rapport. He selects his facts or effects, stylizes and organizes them to correspond with this inner image.

There are, for instance, artists working within the idiom of landscape, who manifest what might be thought of conceptually as a "still-life" attitude. Such an artist *looks on* or *at* nature, separating himself from his environment. This "still-life" painter of landscape tends to be external, to present us head-on with the firm, objective existence of the forms or shapes of what he portrays. He favours solidity and density.

Then there is the artist for whom the coincidence of interior and exterior landscapes results in a sense of identification, a feeling of exultation, of being one with nature, of living *in* nature rather than against it. He does not look on a place, he enters into its space, dwells in it, is absorbed by it. This artist is likely to favour the effect of distance, the illusion of atmosphere, the aura of light, a pictorial depth-space in which the mind can meander and explore.

All of these devices offer a ready attraction to the romantic—though not to him exclusively.

Another attitude might be distinguished—that of the transcendentalist. Here the artist's tendency is toward abstraction, toward holding the form in a timeless, disembodied, crystalline suspension of "absolute" space, a void in which clarified, purely defined forms purged of any deflecting reference to actuality, exist in a serene cosmic vacuum bathed in a "light that never was on land or sea." The only example of this in British Columbia, in its pure form, was in the abstractions of Lawren Harris but which had an influence on both Emily Carr and Jock Macdonald. Varley had previously experimented with the notion in a romantic way.

Vary rarely in British Columbia art (or in Canadian art in general for that matter) is there a manifestation of the expressionist approach to landscape painting in which the externals of subject matter tend to become swept up and absorbed into the artist's sensory neurological gut responses.

But cutting through all these possible approaches there exists another position which is the prerogative of any mature artist whatever his temperamental predilection or attitude. There is the artist for whom the ultimate over-riding concern is for the objective existence of the painting itself, subject to its own intrinsic necessities. It is in this mental territory that the abstractionists have tended to locate their rationale, but the objectivity to which I refer has no reference to any particular idiom but is operable in any of them. Its concern is with the picture plane itself and its own inexorable demands. It confronts us with this invisible plane by insisting upon a clear definition of the negative shape intervals between the positive shapes of the objects and it firmly interlocks these shape-and-interval interactions across the surface. It is less concerned with picturesque illusions of verisimilitude, or seeming volumetric reality, of foreground, middle distance and distance than with pictorial realities of measurable space, tangible surface and the concrete existence of formal interplay. Its regard is for the validity of "experience translated into form" which scrutinizes both the quality of an experience and the authenticity of the form which it generates. The degree of this recognition by the artist is the sign of his command.

So for the keen art watcher there is an extra dividend to this survey beneath this historical record. It is fascinating to detect the play between letting the pictorial space slide toward the horizon, dissolving the picture plane, and the cunning to arrest this flow by an interlocking of space shapes across the surface. Taming the vast space of nature to the mental notions of the painted work and the shaping of the images of our romance to pictorially viable terms and emotionally durable experiences is the hidden record—and closer than one at first thinks to the internal reality of life on the coastal frontier which still powerfully asserts its presence.

Happily, this book which so admirably fills a void in the recording of our cultural history previously neglected invites other volumes, touching divergent problems while adding to our perspective of landscape and art in British Columbia.

JACK SHADBOLT
Vancouver, B.C.
September, 1976

Chapter 1   Early Views: The Eighteenth-Century Exploration

Landscape art in British Columbia began with European discovery. While the West Coast Indians of Canada possessed a remarkable art that became yet more remarkable following the acquisition of tools from trade with Europeans, native art never dealt with the land and seldom portrayed its flora. Landscape art was a European conception and the early Europeans who explored the waters along the northwest coast of North America brought with them well-defined ideas of what landscape should be.[1]

Along the coast south of today's British Columbia British explorers found a land easily conformable to eighteenth-century ideas of beauty. There the mountains stood well back from the sea, allowing a variety of hill and dale "agreeably interspersed with wood-land, and clear spots."[2] The coastline of Washington and Oregon, with its extensive prospects, gradual variation and diver-

16

sity of woods and meadows, provided a close approximation to the artfully landscaped beauty of English parks.

In Puget Sound the entire scene seemed to have been as deliberately planned as the noble estates of Europe. The land rose gently to the snow-capped mountains beyond. Though covered with "a variety of stately forest trees," these did not create "one uninterrupted wilderness, but pleasingly clothed its eminences, and chequered the vallies."[3] Protection Island, off Port Townsend, captivated Captain George Vancouver. Variable elevations, luxuriant grass and abundant flowers were diversified further by occasional clumps of trees. It would have taxed the ingenuity of a landscape designer to arrange them more agreeably. The view was "almost as enchantingly beautiful as the most elegantly finished pleasure ground in Europe." Such scenes required "only to be enriched by the industry of man," with mansions, cottages and villages, "to render it the most lovely country that can be imagined."[4]

North of Burrard Inlet and Juan de Fuca Strait no such artful arrangements were evident. The foreshore of today's British Columbia disappeared as the mountains rose directly from the sea, creating steep cliffs around deep inlets. No longer were there gently ascending hills chequered with varied woodlands, but only conifer-clad mountains rising precipitously above the snowline. The scene lacked all the qualities of the familiar and beautiful. No greater departure from the sensitively arranged nobleman's park could be imagined.

Vancouver found no pleasure in these waters. Anchored along the coast in June, 1792, he despaired of the scene about him. "Our residence here," he wrote, "was truly forlorn."[5] John Meares, a trader, found that the coast was almost totally without variety; it was nothing but "immense ranges of mountains or impenetrable forests."[6] His partner, George Dixon, simply condemned it as "dreary and inhospitable."[7] The British Columbia coast loomed silent and desolate, enveloped by huge and rocky mountains, filled with raging waterfalls and tempestuous weather and frequently obscured by mists and fogs. While this shoreline appeared neither pleasing nor beautiful to the early explorers, it could provide the refined mind of the age with a suitable setting for a study of the sublime in nature.

The sublime was an important concept of eighteenth-century taste. Physical phenomena were sublime when, by darkness, silence, vastness and grandeur, they seized the imagination and stretched its powers; when they inspired and elevated the soul or when they struck awe and a "delightful terror" into the mind of the spectator. Vancouver, who barely appreciated such awesomeness, did admit to the sublimity of Howe Sound, but he found it repellent. To him the entire region seemed dreary and comfortless. In Desolation Sound he found a fitting name for the area that wore "as gloomy and dismal an aspect as nature could well be supposed to exhibit."[8] Archibald Menzies, Vancouver's naturalist, found the coast more capable of emotional uplift. He liked its fathomless inlets, the immensity of its mountains, the perpetuity of its snows. Even the continuous presence of pinery aroused sentiment, however oppressive, and inspired him to contemplate the limitless in nature. The waterfalls, the immense cataracts whose furious wildness "beggered all description," sent a shudder of giddiness through him. The country diffused a "solitary gloom" fitted for the melancholy mood. The rugged, bold and lofty mountains, the surging foam and the high cascading falls, seemed to evoke a feeling of vastness and power that was "favourable to meditation."[9]

European exploration of British Columbia, begun by Juan Pérez in 1774, gained momentum with Captain James Cook's landing at Nootka Sound in 1778. Cook, who had already voyaged twice to the South Pacific, sailed again in 1776 under instructions to search the North Pacific for the elusive Northwest Passage. As it was standard practice to produce from voyages journalistic records for an eighteenth-century public intrigued by accounts of travel to the ends of the world, exploratory voyages usually carried aboard at least one person capable of recording, in line and wash, the curious and the spectacular. Cook, whose voyages were partly scientific and linked closely with Joseph Banks and the Royal Society, carried professional artists on all of his travels. On his third voyage, the only one to touch British Columbia, he again engaged a professional artist, John Webber. The surgeon's mate, William Ellis, was

18

employed as a second artist to be concerned largely with drawing plants and animals.

Webber, as Cook wrote, "was pitched upon ... for the express purpose of supplying the unavoidable imperfections of written accounts, by enabling us to preserve, and to bring home, such drawings of the most memorable scenes of our transactions, as could be expressed by a professed and skilled artist."[10] Born in London in 1751, Webber was sent to Berne as a child to begin his formal art instruction. After further study in Paris he returned to London and in 1776 he exhibited at the Royal Academy, where his work caught the attention of the organizers of Cook's voyage. Webber was engaged as artist on the *Resolution* "to make drawings and paintings of places she may touch on, at a payment of 100 guineas a year."[11] His approach was "essentially illustrative"[12] rather than interpretive.

Webber earned his pay. The products of his pencil are enormous in quantity and are now scattered in a dozen collections on three continents. At Nootka he executed his task as sedulously as elsewhere, drawing coastal profiles, natives and their habitations and implements, and a few general views. Indian subjects were his chief preoccupation. Webber, like other Europeans, was entranced by the exotic and the curious, which at Nootka meant Indians and not, as in the South Pacific, a strange landscape and flora. The village of Yuquot, where Webber made "drawings of every thing that was curious both within and without doors,"[13] was of far greater pictorial interest than the monotonous forest and bare mountains. Landscape was incidental, supplementary or subordinate to the peculiarities of the natives. Only in his striking general view, "*Resolution* and *Discovery* in Nootka Sound," does the landscape become more than a mere backdrop. Terrifying and desolate in its overpowering presence, the terrain is an inhospitable barrier to man. The ships and sailors, even the natives, are active only on the coastal fringe. The rocks and the forest rear up as walls, overwhelming the fragile human endeavour. The *Resolution* and the *Discovery* anchored in the foreground present themselves as solid, reassuring signs of civilization and calm under the great banner of the British ensign. Even here, however, one feels that Webber is

John Webber, *Resolution and Discovery in Nootka Sound,* 1778, watercolour, 23½ x 58½. National Maritime Museum, London, on loan from the Ministry of Defence (Navy).

William Ellis, *View of Ship Cove in King George's Sound, on the N.W. Coast of America,* 1778, watercolour, 13 x 18¾. National Library of Australia, Canberra.

View of Ship Cove, in King George's Sound, in the N.W. Coast of America.

not primarily concerned with the landscape; it is essentially an historical painting, showing the expedition and the natives which are the main subjects of its curiosity. The artist may feel the sublime at Ship Cove, but he does not attempt to point it. If awe-struck or melancholy when contemplating the landscape, he does not convey this emotion onto paper. He is too busy with Nootka types, with interiors of Yuquot houses, with the variety of exotic artifacts, even with a captured sea otter, to concern himself with an essentially forlorn and repellent landscape.

William Ellis,
*A Rock, and a Distant View in
King George's Sound, N.W. Coast
of America*, 1778,
watercolour, 11¼ x 9½.
National Library of Australia,
Canberra.

Webber's fellow artist on the expedition, William Ellis, was not a professional. A Cambridge man, he was educated in medicine at St. Bartholomew's and, according to David Samwell, first mate of the *Resolution,* was "a genteel young fellow and of a good education."[14] Serving as surgeon's mate, Ellis seconded Webber's recording in a less refined but perhaps more interesting way. His attempts at views, as in a Ship Cove drawing, reveal an inability to reproduce the coastal trees. Unlike Webber, whose Swiss background undoubtedly provided him with schemata for coniferous foliage, Ellis drew trees in the only way he knew. Yet in "A Rock and a Distant View" Ellis, perhaps by borrowing from Webber's formula, was able to provide a closer approximation to the western fir.

Captain Vancouver's voyage carried no professional artist. When he took command of the *Discovery,* he noted: "it was with infinite satisfaction that I saw, amongst the officers and young gentlemen of the quarter-deck, some who, with little instruction, would soon be enabled to construct charts, take plans of bays and harbours, draw landscapes, and make faithful portraits of the several headlands, coasts, and countries, which we might discover ... without the assistance of professional persons, as astronomers or draftsmen."[15] Their "on the spot" views were eventually redrawn in London by the professional William Alexander.

Indian villages dominate the published engravings from Vancouver's voyage. Although there are a number of landscape views among the monochrome originals, these convey an impression of dull monotony interspersed by occasional views of "remarkable" rocks or picturesque waterfalls. The perception of a dreary and inhospitable British Columbia is more evident in these simple drawings than in any others.

Spurred by the efforts of Cook and his followers, the Spanish government sent three expeditions north from California. Alejandro Malaspina's 1791 expedition carried two artists, Thomás de Suría, a professional artist-engraver employed at the Mexican mint, and José Cardero, "a simple amateur, not devoid of taste and artistic feeling."[16] Cardero returned to British Columbia in 1792 with expeditions led by Galiano and Valdéz, and in the same year Juan

Francisco de la Bodega y Quadra arrived off the British Columbia coast. Accompanying him was the artist Atanasio Echeverría y Godoy. Echeverría was a young man who possessed, Menzies wrote, "great merit" as a natural history painter.[17]

The three Spanish artists, like Webber and Ellis, were more concerned with native and naturalist subjects than with interpreting the landscape. Like the English artists, their difficulty or diffidence in rendering the conifer became particularly pronounced when their drawings were copied or engraved by other hands. Ellis, as mentioned, had had difficulty with his firs, although Webber, with an Alpine boyhood, was far more familiar with a coniferous landscape than many Englishmen. Conifers, according to prevailing aesthetics, were not beautiful trees. Their "dark murky hue" asso-

James Heath, after H. Humphries and William Alexander, *Friendly Cove, Nootka Sound, V.I.,* engraving, 6 x 9-1/6. From George Vancouver, *A Voyage of Discovery to the North Pacific Ocean, and Round the World* (London: G.G. and J. Robinson, 1798), opposite p.388. Photo: University of British Columbia.

ciated them with the dreary and mournful. Moreover, there were few opportunities to draw them in England and Spain. The artist and engraver of an illustration for Nathaniel Portlock created what could only be palm trees just north of Sitka.[18]

José Cardero, as author of the *Relación del Sutil y Mexicana*, left a written description of the British Columbia landscape as well as his drawings. His impressions of the narrow channels that indent the coast are like those of Vancouver and Menzies. He too noted that, in contrast to Puget Sound, the British Columbia coast did not possess "that pleasant view which the diversity of trees and young plants presents, nor the elegance of flowers and beauty of fruits, nor the variety of quadrupeds and birds." Yet sublimity could be experienced:

> The observer will not fail to find many opportunities to admire the works of nature and divert his thoughts by contemplating the enormous masses of mountains, clad with pines and crowned with snow, which when it melts forms most lovely cascades, and these arriving at the end of their course with amazing velocity, break the silence of these solitudes.[19]

The overland fur traders were generally more spare in their descriptions of the mainland's interior than were sea voyagers about the coast. Those who penetrated the province from the east rarely recorded an impression aside from describing the difficulties of travelling through the terrain. However, like the early explorers who came upon British Columbia by way of the sea, the inland travellers sometimes reacted strongly to the immensity of the wilderness. Alexander Mackenzie, ascending the first mountain after leaving Bentinck Arm, could not help but contemplate the wonder below him. "Such was the depth of the precipices below, and the height of the mountains above, with the rude and wild magnificence of the scenery around," that he could give no adequate description of "such an astonishing and awful combination of objects."[20]

It was David Thompson who drew the first known sketches of the Rockies and the Selkirks. "For these four years," he wrote in 1811, "I have occasionally sketched off various parts of the bold, lofty scenery of the Rocky Mountains about twenty different views,

José Cardero,
Vista del Puerto Nuñez Gaona,
1791,
watercolour, 10½ x 16⅛.
Museo Naval, Madrid.

part on the east side of the Mountains, and also Mount Nelson [the Selkirks], which stands alone in native grandeur. ..."[21] His drawings offer a simple analysis of mountain form and structure. Simon Fraser, whose trip from Fort George to the mouth of the Fraser was as difficult as any of the age, noted that the deep and turbid river which now bears his name gave him a feeling of awe that was not simply a vicarious and controlled terror. The river, scarcely thirty yards in breadth as it passed between precipices, gave an appearance that was "awful to behold!" But the scenery was scarcely elevating to Fraser's soul. His river was nothing but "a continual series of cascades, mixt with rocky fragments and bound by precipices and mountains, that seemed at times to have no end." Fraser's response to such landscape parallels Vancouver's reaction to Desolation Sound. "I scarcely ever saw any thing so dreary," Fraser

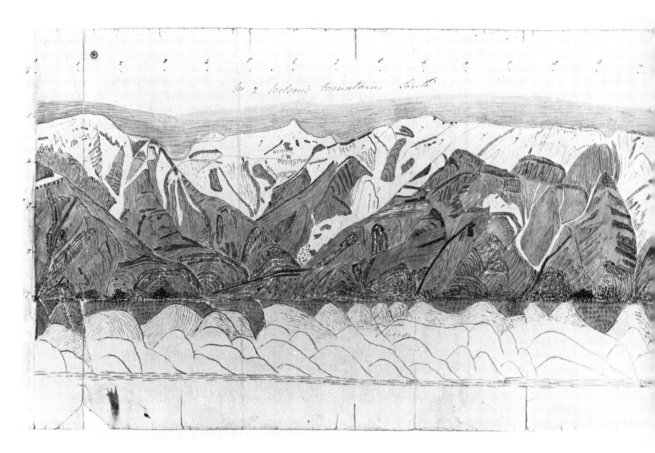

wrote, "and seldom so dangerous in any country; and at present while I am writing this, whatever way I turn, mountains upon mountains, whose summits are covered with eternal snows, close to the gloomy scene."[22] The province's interior was as dreary as its coastline.

The early explorers and fur traders viewed landscape through eyes conditioned to the European taste of their age. Their preference was for extensive vistas with gentle hills, luxuriant meadows interspersed with clumps of trees and the glimpse of a cottage or mansion. Their ideal of beautiful landscape was that of the graciously designed English garden, the informal parks of the landed rich. British Columbia's coastal region scarcely met this standard of beauty. With its enclosed fiords, its rocks and moun-

David Thompson,
No. 2 Nelson's Mountains South,
ca. 1810,
ink and wash, 9 x 13½.
Thomas Fisher Rare Book Library, University of Toronto.

tains, its everlasting conifers, the province struck the eighteenth-century European as desolate. Although the sensitive soul could appreciate it as a suitable setting for the contemplation of melancholy and sublime immensity, generally the region was considered too dreary and monotonous to be beautiful. Inland, the rugged terrain was at least as terrifying to its first explorers and it too appeared overwhelming and awful. The eighteenth-century European simply could not reconcile this rugged and formidable country with his preconceptions of landscape beauty because it was so desolate and inhospitable to human occupation. Native Indians, while exotic and useful trading partners, could not replace browsing cattle or the smoke of cottage chimneys.

Chapter 2   Illustration and Reportage: The Colonial Scene 1843-85

In the early summer of 1842 James Douglas of the Hudson's Bay Company made a careful survey of the southern end of Vancouver Island. This area was already understood to be the most suitable site for the establishment of a post that would eventually replace Fort Vancouver. Douglas' reconnaissance was successful and on March 14, 1843, the *Beaver* anchored at Camosun Bay, the site for the new post.

The choice of Camosun, soon renamed Victoria, was prompted by aesthetic as well as practical factors. A strategic commercial location, a secure harbour and access to timber, water power and agricultural land were primary considerations, but so too was the pleasantness of the location. "The place itself," Douglas wrote, "appears a perfect 'Eden,' in the midst of the dreary wilderness of the Northwest coast, and so different is its general aspect, from the wooded rugged regions around, that one might be pardoned for supposing it had dropped from the clouds into its present position." Douglas was impressed by "this singular District" where the dense and gloomy woods backed off from the shoreline, the surface undulated into hill and dale, and meadows of knee-deep clover, grass and fern were "rendered strikingly picturesque by groups of fir and oaks."[1]

Douglas' report is eloquent testimony to the continued feeling of "dreary wilderness" experienced by Europeans along most of the coast, and to the relief of having found one area "the size of a goodly Parish in the land of cakes"[2] where parkland rather than forest prevailed. This was Victoria's distinction. Her setting was a natural park, so luxuriant in oak and fern, so dotted with hazel, willow, poplar and alder, that "one could hardly believe that this was not the work of art." The eye of the Englishman still desired evidence of man's presence in landscape. "Houses, cleared land, and symptoms of attention and labour," wrote one early visitor, "wonderfully improve a landscape."[3] Victoria's parklands, reminiscent "of some of the noble domains at home,"[4] provided an appearance of artifice to offset the wildness of nature. Similar "smiling tracts" of open prairie where oak and maple, not fir, predominated[5] were soon discovered, but these only made greater the contrast of the surrounding landscape. The general appearance of Vancouver Island was, to its first non-company settler, "peculiarly uninviting": "Dark, frowning cliffs sternly repel the foaming sea, as it rushes impetuously against them, and beyond these, with scarcely any interval of level land, rounded hills, densely covered with firs, rise one above the other in dull uninteresting monotony."[6] This country, lacking all artifice and dominated by the sombre green of primeval forests, was gloomy, thoroughly wild, even savage. It held little attraction with its "everlasting pine-trees."[7] From such regions "which are wild without being romantic, and which, from the absence of any bold outline, never approach to the sublime or the beautiful," the traveller was happy to escape to areas like Victoria,[8] which were more congenial to the tastes of Britons accustomed to a tamed and park-like landscape.

Henry J. Warre,
*H. B. C. Settlement and Fort
Victoria on Vancouvers Island,
Straits Juan de Fuca,* 1845,
watercolour, 6⅞ x 9⅝.
Courtesy of the American
Antiquarian Society,
Worcester, Massachusetts.

Lieutenant Henry J. Warre, a trained though amateur artist who visited Victoria in 1845, found the "alternate masses of wood and small plains" and the "wide open prairies thinly scattered with fine oak trees" pleasantly pretty and picturesque.[9] Most of his sketches, however, have the fort and figures as their subjects. Paul Kane, a Toronto artist who arrived eighteen months later, was even more concerned with human subjects as he made a useful record of Northwest Indians. Kane's published account, *Wanderings of an Artist*, does not demonstrate a vivid sensitivity to landscape. His landscape sketches centre on either the fort or Indian villages and figures. Kane and Warre, working within the conventional attitude of the age, felt at ease only when the landscape was humanized by man or his marks.

The mainland's coast remained as desolate as that of the Island. If anything, wrote one colonist, it was "more forbidding."[10] The mainland's mountains, however, were beginning to be appreciated by a few who came into contact with them. Kane was attracted to the volcanic mountains along the coast, and Warre was struck by the beauty of the Olympic range as it was seen from Victoria, and, above all, by the magnificence of Mount Baker's "milky whiteness."[11]

British Columbia's mountains now began their long period of dominance in landscape perception and art. By the 1840s mountains had lost the genuine terror that had inspired the previous century to its awful contemplation of them. Mountains became the subject of conventionalized emotion and romantic exaggeration. No one in the Victorian era could write of mountains without resorting to rhetorical bombast. A sense of genuine awe dissolved into a feigned sensationalism. The British lieutenant's writing and the Toronto artist's pictures demonstrate the conventionalized mountain glory that accompanied Victorian aesthetics.

Warre, returning to Montreal via the Athabasca Pass, was genuinely impressed by the country. In his private journal he confessed that it was beyond his power to describe the view at Boat Encampment. The almost total lack of inhabitants, even Indians, lent a desolation which added grandeur to the wildly beautiful scenes of the pass. Mountain rose above mountain, each capped and clothed in a dazzling winter mantle. Although his diary descriptions of desolate beauty are kept in reserved perspective and are genuine and convincing, Warre's published narrative is quite different. Here he invests the scene with a much more dramatic power. Climbing over the pass, he found the view "awful in its savage solitude":

> Not a vestige of human life to be seen, ney! so far as we knew existed for miles around. ... The scenery through which we passed onward was grand beyond description—but oh how desolate! Mountains upon mountains reared their naked heads high above the mists, which rolled upwards from the valley below: pine & fir trees

Henry J. Warre, *The Rocky Mountains of British Columbia from the Columbia River looking North West*, 1845, watercolour on tinted paper, 10⅜ x 15¾. The Public Archives of Canada.

Paul Kane, *Encampment, Foot of the Rocky Mountains*, 1846, watercolour, 5¼ x 8¾. Courtesy of the Stark Foundation of Orange, Texas.

Encampment Foot of the Rocky Mountains

Paul Kane,
Boat Encampment, ca. 1850,
oil on canvas, 18 x 29¼.
Royal Ontario Museum,
Toronto.

broken by storms & wonderfully picturesque in shape grew together
in the ravines or stood like sentinels scattered amidst the rugged
rocks. The trackless vallies were smooth with unbroken snow. No
living thing dared to brave the awful loneliness . . .[12]

Thrown into this theatrical narrative are thundering avalanches
over whose still-quivering remains they were forced to pass,
"expecting every hour to be buried in the ruins."[13]

Such romantic exaggeration, clichéd and conventional, does
not enter into Warre's drawings and watercolours, nor into the
published lithographs of the journey. His sketches are freshly
honest. The grandeur of the mountains is not exaggerated. In "The
Rocky Mountains of British Columbia from the Columbia River
looking North West" the foreground figures offset as much as they
dramatize the immensity of the mountain background. The picture
is an honest perception, reflecting a picturesque mode untouched
by the bombastic.

Kane, not one easily impressed by landscape, marvelled at the
scenery of the upper Columbia. The "romantic wildness," the
"stupendous and ever-varying" scenery of the river, he wrote,
"exceeds in grandeur any other perhaps in the world."[14] Kane
adapted to his oils the exaggerated sublime that Warre had transferred to his published description. The mountains in the delicate

and delightful watercolour of Boat Encampment are of medium height. In subsequently painting the same subject in oil, Kane invented much grander forms to tower above the human camp.

This conventional mountain sublime is also evident in some of the gold rush descriptions of the mainland. Brought into rushed familiarity with the mountainous interior, Europeans quickly made a legend of the ruggedness of the landscape as they struggled up the Fraser. Most of the miners rarely gave much attention to the scenery and less to describing it, but one John Emmerson of Wolsingham was influenced by the rhetoric of the Victorian sublime. In the interior Emmerson found himself surrounded by "immense mountains of the most wild and awe-inspiring description." It was "a wild, romantic, mountainous country," with "grand and impressive" scenery. Frequently, wrote Emmerson, "we were brought to a dead stop—struck with wonder and amazement on viewing those gigantic mountains."[15] Others, seeing the scenery as "romantically beautiful" or "eminently picturesque," compared the mountains at Hope to the Scottish Highlands or felt that Harrison Lake was quite Alpine in character.[16] But old-world comparisons were inadequate to the "wild and terrible character" of the Fraser Canyon. Characteristic is R.C. Mayne's description:

> Looking up between the precipitous cliffs, the water is seen rushing through them at fearful speed. I hardly know which was more grand, the view from this spot or that further on, as we got well into the cañon, in which in places the trail led up crags so steep that we had to clamber up them with our hands and feet, until we arrived breathless at the top of a projecting ledge, on which we were glad to halt a few minutes, to draw breath and gaze with wonder on the scene.[17]

This was the conventional sublime, contrived and exaggerated. The mountains of British Columbia, which the eighteenth-century maritime explorers had seen largely at a distance or, when enclosed in an inlet, as hindrances to a vista, and which the land explorers had seen as obstacles, now came into the everyday view of settlers and visitors. Their majesty, almost universally appreciated, was vested with theatrical fear and terror and occasionally with a Ruskin morality. The dominant aspect of the landscape was now its mountains. Edmund T. Coleman's 1868 essay "On the Beauties of the Scenery as Surveyed from Beacon Hill"[18] demonstrates the mountain primacy and the Victorian aesthetic behind it.

Coleman was a Londoner, sometime exhibitor of historical and landscape pictures at the Royal Academy and a member of the Alpine Club of London. He spent four consecutive seasons in the Alps, climbed Mont Blanc twice, and published *Scenes from the Snow-Fields* in 1858, a description of the "Upper Ice-World" with nineteen colour lithographs, some of which are of spectacular beauty. Coleman arrived in Victoria in 1863 as a gold seeker, although he seems never to have travelled to the fields. When the Literary Institute offered a prize for the best essay on Beacon Hill's vista, Coleman wrote the winning piece.

The essay is a rare document, a serious and philosophical essay rather than an emigrant tract or a travel journal. The author noted, of course, the unexcelled panoramic position of Beacon Hill, but it was the mountain scenery that most impressed him. While ordinary scenes—the woods and the dale, the gentle slope and the winding river—conveyed to Coleman "soothing and agreeable images," only mountain scenery could "touch those deeper chords, and awaken those grander sensations, which it is one of the highest privileges of our nature to feel." Thus Beacon Hill's vista, while it encompassed hills and valleys, rugged cliffs and sloping ground, woodland and forest, "the smiling city and the mighty ocean," displayed above all those conspicuously "towering masses": "No one can survey these magnificent peaks, arrayed in virgin white, that have stood from all time with their foundations deeply laid in the earth, emblems of stability and power, without some emotion of awe and wonder, and without being for a while spell bound and exalted."[19]

Coleman's reaction to the mountains reflected the conventional sublime, but the exaltation with which he invested them conveyed a moralistic view of landscape and nature that characterized post-Wordsworth Victorian views. The love of nature, Coleman wrote, "is one of the most refining and elevating emotions of which man is capable," an emotion which becomes "an exalting exercise of mind" leading upward from nature to nature's God. It was fitting, therefore, that he should conclude his essay on a high moral and religious tone; the aims of his fellow townsmen should be as lofty as the mountains, their resolves as steadfast as the hills, their desires as pure as those snows, and their thoughts "lifted to the land where flowers forever bloom."[20]

Unfortunately, few examples of Coleman's own drawings are available. The engravings for his article "Mountaineering on the Pacific" do convey a feeling of awesome and desolate splendour, but they are schematic line engravings designed to enliven the text of a popular monthly.[21] One of his two known drawings is a commissioned picture of Alexandra Bridge, done for its proud builder,

Edmund T. Coleman,
Alexandra Bridge, ca. 1863,
pencil, 8 x 11.
Provincial Archives, Victoria,
B.C.

Joseph Trutch. An exact side view, the bridge dominates without enhancing the dully conceived landscape around it. An Indian canoe, almost a cliché in colonial pictures, provides the necessary human interest.

Between Paul Kane's visit and the arrival of artists from eastern Canada and abroad in the 1880s, there was little artistic concern in British Columbia. The small company-dominated settlements at Victoria, Nanaimo, Kamloops and Langley produced nothing more than the rare Sunday amateur. However, the gold rush brought with it a number of immigrants who happened also to be picture makers. By the 1860s numerous pictures were being painted—by naval officers, by artistic adventurers and by the very occasional amateur of the more cultivated settler class. In almost all cases, however, the painted picture was less an expression of artistic vision than a topographical illustration or a pictorial souvenir. One exception, so formidable that it deserves special attention, was the work of William George Richardson Hind, who came to the gold fields and Victoria with the Overlanders of 1862.

During the winter of 1861-2 news of gold discoveries in the Cariboo prompted William Redgrave of Toronto to organize a group of gold seekers, adventurers and an artist, W.G.R. Hind, on an expedition to the Cariboo gold fields. Travelling from Toronto via St. Louis and St. Paul to Fort Garry, they constructed the famous Red River carts which took them to the foot of the Rockies. From there they trekked by foot and pack horse to the Cariboo.

This was not Hind's first experience as an expedition artist since arriving in Canada from Nottingham, England, in 1851. In 1861 he had accompanied his brother, Henry Youle Hind, to Labrador. The Cariboo trek did not result in coloured lithographs and etchings to accompany an official report, as on the Labrador expedition, but in watercolours and sketches depicting buffalo on the plains, despondent miners in a Barkerville bar and weary donkeys making their way along the treacherous Cariboo trail.

Considered by some to be a primitive, Hind reputedly studied both in London and on the Continent before joining his brother in Upper Canada where he took a position as professor of drawing at the Toronto Normal School. Before the Overlanders' trek he had

W.G.R. Hind, *Wood Interior with Tree Stump,* ca. 1863, watercolour, 7 x 8¾. Private Collection.

made a brief visit to England at a time when the art of William Holman Hunt and other Pre-Raphaelites was in vogue. Though his landscape detail, "Wood Interior with Tree Stump," reflects the closely packed, detailed paintings of the Pre-Raphaelites, and his genre subjects possess a stop-action quality derived from photography, many of his Rocky Mountain landscape sketches have a much looser rendering. He often concentrated on foreground detail, allowing the broader aspects of the landscape to emerge incidentally. This was a radical departure from the inclination of his contemporaries to moralize or feign contemplation of a panoramic view. More primitive, with its stiff figures, two-dimensional perspective and bold colours is "At the Foot of the Rocky Mountains." This view of the eastern side of the Rockies also possesses the Pre-Raphaelite absence of shadow and love of detail. Every blade of grass, every branch, is meticulously painted.

Hind's versatility was put to good use when he took a studio in Victoria in 1863. J. Russell Harper writes that "Hind was part of the lively local art scene in Victoria."[22] In addition to working up many of his Overland sketches and watercolours into oils, he painted commercial signs, portraits and the local scenery.

Even Hind found that in colonial British Columbia art was the most tertiary of professions. The coastal colonies were, noted the *Colonist*, "a very limited community for a professional landscape painter."[23] An ability to recreate a scene on paper was, nevertheless, an occasionally useful skill for the surveyor, the civil engineer and the architect; it remained, until photogravure became common in the 1880s, the basis for engraved illustration. Joseph Despard Pemberton, surveyor for the Island colony, found his sketching ability a practical asset, and H. D. Teidemann, architect and civil engineer, was a competent draughtsman, contributing a topographical panoramic engraving of Victoria that suffered considerable embellishment when re-engraved by a London firm.

Artists were normally included in exploratory expeditions in much the same way as Webber had served Cook and young lieutenants sketched for Vancouver. An example of this, as well as of the quite practical role an artist played in such society, was the employment of an illustrator by the 1864 expedition to explore the interior of Vancouver Island.

When the idea of engaging an artist to accompany the expedition was mooted, competition was intense between three underemployed artists in Victoria. Coleman sought the post on the strength of his physical stamina, twice proven on Mont Blanc, his commissions from Trutch, and his Alpine sketches for *Scenes from the Snow-Fields*.[24] E.M. Richardson drew attention to his three years of study under Sir George Hayter at the Royal Academy and his sketches in the Cariboo, but, more practically, pointed out that he was also an experienced surveyor.[25] Frederick Whymper, the successful applicant, left no stone unturned in his quest for the position. He bombarded the committee with letters, calling upon his engraving experience in his father's London workshop, offering sample sketches, referring the committee to Lord Milton, Judge Begbie, Archdeacon Wright and the Rev. Sheepshanks as persons in a position "to testify to the faithfulness of my pencil."[26]

In fact, Whymper was particularly suitable for such an expeditionary role. The son of Josiah Wood Whymper, a highly successful London wood engraver, he had learned drawing and

W.G.R. Hind,
At the Foot of the Rocky
Mountains, 1862-3,
watercolour, 8½ x 12.
McCord Museum, Montreal.

engraving as part of the discipline of his father's Lambeth studio. More ambitiously, he began to submit pictures to Royal Academy shows in 1859, but this career of painting in Surrey and on the Seine was interrupted in 1862 when the call of the Cariboo gold rush led him to book passage for Victoria. The arrival of spring took him to the mainland for a sketching and pedestrian tour of the gold fields.[27] He did sketches for claimholders and mining companies, and, back in Victoria for the winter of 1863-4, showed the editors of the *Colonist* "some very neat water-color sketches of scenes in Cariboo and along the wagon road."[28] Never idle long, in March he was engaged by Alfred Waddington "to take sketches of the grand scenery which is to be found along the Bute route, with the intention of sending them to London."[29] Whymper was greatly impressed by the superb scenery of the Homothco Canyon and the mountains, but what interested him most were the great glaciers. He spent days observing and sketching them, then hurried back to Victoria with his pictures and news of Indian unrest. While the colonial governments mounted a campaign against the Indian uprising, Whymper showed his sketches to a gratified *Colonist* which was most impressed by "the grand scenery" and by the pictures which served to give "a better idea of the nature of the country than all the verbal descriptions yet published."[30] As the successful applicant to the Island exploratory expedition, Whymper departed with the party for the mouth of the Cowichan in June, 1864. The trip offered the kind of adventure in which Whymper revelled. Days of toil and hardship, wading in streams, tramping through the dense growth, "cooning" along slippery logs, walking through drenching downpours heavily loaded with instruments and provisions, the expedition tested the manliness of an adventurous Londoner while providing unforgettable camaraderie around the evening camps, when "a good log-fire, a bed of fir-brush, and a pipe made us happy."[31] Exploring from Cowichan to Nitinat, from Port Renfrew to Nanaimo and across the Island to Barkley Sound, the party found a few coal seams, little agricultural land, and enough gold to spark the Leechtown rush. With the Cariboo, Bute Inlet and the interior of Vancouver Island behind him, Whymper was ready for further sketching adventures. The following spring

E.M. Richardson,
Inner Harbour, Victoria, ca. 1864,
watercolour, 7 x 14.
Provincial Archives, Victoria, B.C.

he left Victoria as artist to the Collins Overland telegraph scheme in Russian America.

Whymper, who with his father and brothers had engraved the illustrations for Livingstone's *Travels* and the Alpine Club's *Peaks and Passes*, was pre-eminently an illustrator. His strong outlines were easily transformed into published form for several books on British Columbia and the Yukon and for the *Illustrated London News*. The drawings seldom depart from the topographical, though his delicate use of washes, as in a sketch of Fort Yale, do give indisputable charm to a picturesque view of a struggling settlement cozily settled along its river and almost protected by its magnificent mountain background.

Coleman, Whymper and Richardson were not the only artists of the illustrative and topographical style active in the coastal colo-

Frederick Whymper,
Fort Yale, British Columbia,
1864,
watercolour, 7 x 9.
Provincial Archives, Victoria,
B.C.

F.G.D. Bedford,
Esquimalt from anchorage H.M.S.
Shah, June 22, 1878, 1878,
watercolour, 3 x 13⅜.
Provincial Archives, Victoria,
B.C.

nies. The international boundary survey brought several practitioners of this tradition. The Collins telegraph used John C. White
of the Royal Engineers and Franklin L. Pope from New York in
addition to Whymper. As important, the gradual establishment of
the Royal Navy at Esquimalt meant the presence of a large number
of naval officers trained in drawing. Draughtsmanship was a valu-
able skill in the navy, continually emphasized by an Admiralty
interested in men qualified to provide sketches of ports, anchorages
and coastal profiles. This topographical convention dominates the
naval pictures. They are "place-portraits" of Craigflower, of Roche
Harbour, of Nanaimo, or simple marine pictures portraying ships
like the H. M. S. Plumper steaming through coastal waters. In these
there is little art, no vision and sparse imagination. The landscape
is captured as it is, uninspired and unembellished. Frederick G. D.
Bedford's "Esquimalt from anchorage H. M. S. Shah" is an extreme
example of literal treatments, in its precise, prosaic representation
of the coastal panorama.

Throughout most of the nineteenth century, landscape art in
British Columbia continued in the European tradition. The early
colonists continued to be impressed by tamed vistas, parkland
surroundings and evidence of human endeavour and, with the
exception of a few favoured areas such as Victoria, the spectacular
terrain of the West Coast was still seen as gloomy and forbidding.
By this time, however, some visitors had begun to appreciate the

immensity and grandeur of the western mountains. No longer as terrifying or inaccessible, the mountains were now portrayed in terms as lavish and bombastic as the Victorian sensibility could express. Many looked to them for moral uplift and emotional exaltation—as a means of reaching God through nature.

In this period, navy draughtsmen, gold seekers and artists on exploratory expeditions had begun to depict the topographical features of British Columbia in a style that was primarily illustrative and documentary. Naval exploration carried on to the end of the century, but with the collapse of the gold rush, the colonies suffered a precipitous decline. In the 1870s and early 1880s they ceased to attract artistic adventurers like Hind, Whymper and Coleman. Landscape art awaited a new infusion of ideas and techniques which would continue the mountain dominance, but would also lead to the founding of a settled community of landscape artisans. They would begin their own gradual development of a recognizable British Columbia tradition.

Chapter 3   Pursuing the Exotic: Late Nineteenth-Century Visitors

In the late 1880s British Columbia became the scene for an enormous output of landscape pictures painted by central Canadians. In 1871 the Pacific colony somewhat reluctantly joined the recently confederated Dominion of Canada. For British Columbia this promised a release from post-gold rush stagnation through the building of a railway east. For the rest of Canada it meant a Pacific connection, a part of the westward expansion which had brought Manitoba and the Northwest Territories to the Dominion in 1870. Canadian artists were quick to respond to the western impulse.

Led by William Armstrong, who accompanied Colonel Wolseley's expedition to the Red River in 1870, and by F.A. Verner, who developed a life-long interest in depicting the western Indians and mist-shrouded buffalo, artists from central Canada penetrated into the prairie West. As the Pacific Railway advanced, Thomas

Mower Martin followed it to the Lake Superior region in 1882; in the same year Lucius O'Brien travelled from Chicago to the Canadian Rockies on horseback. A.P. Coleman, a professional geologist and amateur painter, sketched in the Rocky Mountains the following year. These were only the vanguard of a host of European and eastern Canadian painters who were to have an artistic field day in British Columbia after the completion of the Canadian Pacific Railway in 1885.

The railway encouraged the artists, giving them free passes and occasional commissions. Sir William Van Horne, himself a significant collector and connoisseur, was the chief patron, although Lord Mount Stephen also provided passes. Artists were quick to seize upon the possibilities which the Rockies, the Selkirks, the Fraser Canyon, the Pacific coastline and the West Coast Indians offered to their brush. The British Columbia scenery was exhilarating to the small group of professional and semi-professional painters centred in Toronto. The *a mari usque ad mare* ideal of Confederation was now realized and they basked in its glory. Between Cape Breton and Vancouver every kind of scenery could be found—wild, rocky shores, flat and sandy coasts, undulating pastoral lands, thundering waterfalls, gigantic mountains—all were there to be chosen and all had been now made accessible by the trans-continental railway. Sketching in Stanley Park, impressed by the gigantic trees, one artist marvelled that here, nearly three thousand miles from Montreal, "we are still in Canada." "It is," he wrote, "an extensive country, whose magnificent distances we have again to travel over for six days and nights before we can again reach Toronto."[1] Here was the patriotism of the central Canadian, discovering a newer Canada.

The artists revelled in the sights and sensations of this new frontier. Lucius O'Brien, sitting on the front of a locomotive travelling downhill from Rogers Pass, could think of few things to compare with "the sensation of a spin down the Kicking Horse." Camping in the mountains, he exalted, "we were free, free to rough it and be at home with nature."[2] J.A. Fraser was astonished at the "new and strange" beauty of Lytton and Kamloops, and amazed at being able to walk across the Fraser on salmon.[3] All had such stories to tell back home—F.M. Bell-Smith of the sudden and unmannered appearance of a huge bear within a few feet of his easel at Mount Sir Donald, of his horse bolting on the valley trail to Corbin's mine, of brandishing his parasol at a threatening eagle on Asulkan Glacier.[4] Thomas Mower Martin had his tales of the Illecillewaet ice cave, of gigantic forest fires, of the lake he could not find amid the impenetrable forest at Stanley Park.[5] The visitors were exuberant tourists on a busman's holiday, roughing it with their easels at Donald, carting their canvases along the Fraser Canyon, sketching the gigantic trees of Stanley Park, drawing picturesque Indians at Alert Bay. Some, like O'Brien, were content with three trips; others came West year after year. Mower Martin spent ten consecutive summers along the C.P.R., while Bell-Smith came to the Rockies more than twenty times.

This was "the Rocky Mountain period of Canadian painting."[6] Although every kind of scenery could be found in the West, it was the variety and ubiquity of the mountains that interested the late nineteenth-century visitors. The grandeur that had become part of the consciousness of Europeans in the eighteenth century as an awesome and terrifying feeling, the magnificence that had been rhetorically clichéd and moralized by the mid-Victorians, had now been tamed to poetic, even pedestrian, proportions. To the central Canadian and immigrant Englishman, the mountains were merely an intriguing landscape novelty.

Although the conventional wisdom of the time had it that mountains were, save for someone of Turner's genius, impossible to paint, "the imagination of the landscape painters was fired by the ambition to paint the unpaintable."[7] Some artists were rendered impotent before the Rockies. Fraser at first found them indescribable by pen or brush. He told of his first view of the Rockies, how their panorama grew in size and how his astonishment increased at their beauty and splendour: "Up, up, ever up," the train went, "past peak after peak, glaciers innumerable, over madly-roaring boiling torrents, toying with and playfully flinging here and there on their snowy crest, trees." Still up and up, until at the seven-thousand-foot-high base of Mount Stephen, with its peak piercing the clouds still a mile higher, "with head swimming and eyes and neck aching and your heart thumping against your ribs, you cry, enough!"[8] Fraser confessed that painting the mountains was not easy. One of his fellows, he said, "wandered confusedly for many days," while his "hands hung helplessly in the presence of those peaks over which the clouds, with their ever-changing lights and shades, travelled carelessly." Others were less intimidated. "One among us," he recalled, "was a grand example of patient persistence. Although the smoke of eight hundred miles of forest fires hid anything beyond fifty yards, it made no difference: "He had begun his pictures under happier auspices and he faithfully repaired, day in and day out, to his chosen grounds, and 'fired away.'"[9]

Lucius O'Brien was one of the most successful and skilled of these visitors. One of the few prominent native Canadian artists at that time, O'Brien was born of a gentleman's family in Shanty Bay, Ontario, and educated at Upper Canada College. Although trained as an architect and civil engineer, he became a professional painter in the 1870s. O'Brien was within the English tradition, yet influenced by the American romanticism of the Hudson River-Bierstadt school of landscape painters. He brought to British Columbia an ability to paint realistically, and the skill to endow that realism with poetic imagination. O'Brien made an early trip west in 1882, travelling with his missionary brother by horse from Chicago. In 1886 he left Toronto for the first of three painting summers in the West, and in 1887 he accompanied J.C. Forbes and other Ontarians, camping in the mountains under canvas tents. He thoroughly enjoyed the novelty of the outdoor life. Feeling at home with nature, he and the artists with whom he travelled were "attuned, in our life and surroundings, to her wildest mood, and yet not without the comforts of savage life and what we care to have of the resources of civilization."[10] Their roaring fire in the chill night air was a cheery speck among the mountain solitudes. The author-pastor, William Withrow, who visited the group at Glacier, recalled "the glorious camp-fire around which we gathered at night beneath the shadow of the surrounding mountains."[11]

The constantly changing form, colour and atmosphere of the mountains were of inexhaustible interest to O'Brien: "At one

Lucius Richard O'Brien,
A Prospector's Camp, 1887,
watercolour, 10¾ x 14-15/16.
Art Gallery of Ontario, Gift of
Miss Lucy O'Brien, 1920.

moment the mountains seem quite close, masses of rich, strong colour; then they will appear far away, of the faintest pearly gray." "The study of these scenes," he wrote, "in all the wealth of their luxuriant detail, which is requisite in order at all to paint them, is wonderfully interesting and delightful." Yet painting the Rockies was heart-breaking—"so little of all this beauty can be placed upon paper or canvas, and of that little much, I fear, will be incomprehensible to dwellers upon the plains."[12]

O'Brien, perhaps because of his humility, was successful in translating the mountain scene to paper. "A Prospector's Camp" dextrously blends figures and landscape. The mountains, "of the faintest pearly grey," retain an awesome splendour while the human element in the foreground prevents the "unpaintable" mountains from running away with the picture.

On a third railway trip in 1888 O'Brien "resisted all the fascinations of the unexplored places by the way" to fulfil his desire "to see something of the fiords and inlets of the Pacific coast."[13] Again he found subjects in abundance. He hired a canoe and two Indians to paddle him along the coast of Howe Sound where he

Lucius Richard O'Brien,
A British Columbian Forest,
1888,
watercolour, 21½ x 30⅛.
The National Gallery of
Canada, Ottawa.

sketched a number of coastal views of routine and picturesque composition. Somewhere near here, perhaps at his Point Atkinson campsite, he did "A British Columbian Forest," a watercolour that captures the rich, shaded greens of the rain forest interior, but which has also the extravagant flavour of a posed tourist snapshot. "A British Columbia forest, untouched by fire or lumberman's axe, with its enormous trees and wild luxuriant undergrowth," he wrote to a friend in Toronto, "is a sight never to be forgotten; the towering tapering pillars of cedar and fir, rising for a hundred feet and more without a branch, are interspersed with a variety of trees and shrubs of smaller growth, nearly all different to those of our Eastern woods."[14] The words, like the picture, betray the attraction to the exotic and unfamiliar which was felt by a Shanty Bay Ontarian on a summer's trip to the Pacific rain forest. In "A Prospector's Camp" O'Brien had used figures to prevent the mountains from over-whelming the picture; here the gigantic tree and dense mass of ferns and forest undergrowth deliberately overwhelm the tiny figures. O'Brien, typical of many Ontario vagabonds of the 1880s and 90s, was painting postcard views of British Columbia.

Better known than O'Brien was Frederic Marlett Bell-Smith, "premier painter of the Rockies." Born in England in 1846, he came to Canada with his artist father in 1867, living in Montreal, Hamilton and London as well as in Toronto, where he eventually settled. After a brief stay in Europe for study at the Académie Colarossi, he was back in Canada in time to participate in the Rockies rush of the 1880s, making the first of his twenty-odd trips in 1887. It had been, he recalled, one of the dreams of his early manhood to paint the Rocky Mountains: "I dreamed this over and over again until the vision took form." "Very early one summer's morning" he found himself looking at "the vanguard sentinels of the mountain host." There they stood, "displaying the glint of their glacial accoutrements" and beckoning "the enraptured pilgrim to explore their mysteries and their shrines."[15] The rhapsodizing was quite in character. Bell-Smith was a popular and poetic painter. Unlike O'Brien, whose independent income allowed him to spend more time on individual works, Bell-Smith had to live from his art. Mountain pictures were popular, the C.P.R. was liberal with its

54

F.M. Bell-Smith,
Mists and Glaciers of the Selkirks,
1911,
oil on canvas, 33¼ x 49½.
The National Gallery of
Canada, Ottawa.

passes and he possessed a certain show-business talent that helped
to sell his numerous pictures. At his almost annual stopovers in
Victoria he would hold an exhibition of pictures and, to lend added
interest to his art, he sometimes held a "recital." Combining his
gifts as a reader with his artistic talent, he occasionally closed his
exhibitions with a series of "lightning sketches." Such feats
enhanced the artist's popularity, but inevitably fostered a reputation for pandering to popularity and for empty repetition. He was,
wrote one later critic, "essentially an unashamed purveyor of
pictures for the market place, and he would not hesitate to repeat
the identical composition as many times as he could sell it."[16]Even
the most hostile critic must, however, concede the occasional
success. Bell-Smith possessed, along with his remarkable visual
memory and easy ability, a genuine lyrical love for the landscape
of British Columbia. "Mists and Glaciers of the Selkirks" possesses
this poetic quality and makes it one of the outstanding pictures of
the age.

     With Bell-Smith one must mention an artist who spent nearly
as much time in the province. Thomas Mower Martin is the prosaic
poet of these tourists, as repetitive as Bell-Smith but without the

facility of his friend and colleague. With little art training, Mower Martin's watchword, variously expressed, was "put your colors out on your palette and paint what you see."[17] He felt a mission "to interpret the beauties of nature into a language that all can understand."[18] His "Artist's Letter from the Rockies" describes a jaunt from the Prairies to Vancouver, looking at picturesque Hoodoos and Indians, forest fires and ice caves, admiring panoramas, always "searching for new subjects for pictures."[19] Mower Martin is the artist-tourist *par excellence.* Often his landscapes are almost standardized compositions of a central road or stream winding through treed or mountainous sidewings; his output of such pictures was enormous. He later confessed, "I can't remember half of them, I have painted so many."[20] There is the rare gem among his usually pedestrian outpourings. "Ice Cave, Illecillewaet Glacier, B.C." is one, an example of exceptional talent and exotic beauty.

There were numerous other eastern Canadian visitors who came to the Rockies and the coast to see what the railway had made accessible to painterly tourists. They were joined by Englishmen like Edward Roper, who came in 1887 to chronicle his journey "by track and trail through Canada," painting picturesque scenes along the way which served as illustrations to his book.[21] Most of the visiting Europeans were simply tourists, but one couple, the de L'Aubinières, stayed long enough to make a small impact upon the Victoria public.

C.A. de L'Aubinière was a French painter, reputedly a student of Corot and Gérôme. An exhibitor in England, he met and married Georgina Steeple, the daughter of John Steeple, a well-known English watercolourist, and herself a frequent watercolour exhibitor at the Royal Academy. Late in 1886, after a tour of the United States, the couple arrived in Victoria. Touted as distinguished artists whose pictures commanded universal admiration throughout Europe and who were patronized by the Queen, the couple took Victoria society by storm. Their visit to the city coincided with the beginnings of the Queen's Diamond Jubilee celebrations, when the couple was commissioned by the provincial government to paint a series of fourteen oils for royal presentation. Photographs of their pictures and the accompanying illuminated address were offered

▲

Thomas Mower Martin,
Ice Cave, Illecillewaet Glacier,
B.C., no date,
watercolour, 19½ x 13⅝.
Glenbow-Alberta Institute,
Calgary.

Georgina M. de L'Aubinière, ▶
Forest and Swamp, 1887,
watercolour, 10 x 14.
Provincial Archives, Victoria,
B.C.

Edward Roper,
Glacier 90, Selkirks, B.C., 1887,
guache, 26 x 19 (sight).
Private Collection.

to the public for eight dollars, and a large show comprising 150 pictures opened in October. At the same time, C.A. de L'Aubinière proposed to the Colonial Secretary that a Victoria Jubilee Museum and Art School be established in the provincial capital. Victoria, he argued, though not large, had a society "composed of superior and cultivated persons, by whom any movement in favour of the Fine Arts would be warmly welcomed."[22] Nothing came of the idea, but in all other respects the European visitors rather swept Victorians off their feet. The artistic productions of the pair were greatly appreciated and eagerly purchased. The *Colonist* felt that, until their arrival, no realistic pictures of Victoria's natural scenery had been painted.[23] Not all the city reacted this way. Emily Carr, a young girl of fifteen and probably among the students in the de L'Aubinières' classes, later wrote in her characteristically truculent manner:

> I was tremendously awed when a real French artist with an English artist-wife came to Victoria. I expected to see something wonderful, but they painted a few faraway mountains floating in something hazy that was not Canadian air, a Chinaman's shack on which they put a curved roof like an Eastern temple, then they banged down the lids of their paintboxes, packed up, went back to the Old World. Canada had no scenery, they said.[24]

It is more likely that the couple left when the market was saturated and no additional government patronage was forthcoming. They did leave behind more than a few paintings, including one by C.A. de L'Aubinière which has a faraway Mount Baker floating in a haze very familiar today. While C.A. de L'Aubinière's oils are often worthy of Carr's scorn, Georgina de L'Aubinière's watercolours are delicate, even beautiful. They capture the domesticated scenery around Victoria, although they never venture close to coniferous forests or mountains.

Not all the arrivals in British Columbia proved to be transient visitors. The rapid settlement after 1885 brought a number of artists to the province as permanent residents. One early artist-settler was H. Tomtu Roberts who arrived in Vancouver in 1886 from Wales and worked as an artist for a number of years, establishing an art gallery on Cordova Street. Roberts was obviously fascinated by the primeval forests around him, something alien to a Welshman, but

C.A. de L'Aubinière,
Mount Baker from Victoria,
1887,
oil on board, 10 x 14.
Provincial Archives, Victoria,
B.C.

captivating and obsessive. On one remarkable sketch he inscribed notations on how correctly to paint the foliage of a cedar. "Put simple lights & simple shadows then high lights then cool tints in the shadows," he wrote, "& it is done." Roberts, one of the earliest of the mainland's settlers, was searching for an accommodation of his traditional style to aspects of the landscape that were new to his experience.

The late nineteenth century saw the opening of the transcontinental railway and a great influx of settlers and exuberant artists to the West Coast from Europe and eastern Canada. The artists were fascinated by the novel elements of the mountain terrain and the luxuriance of the province's rain forests, and they pursued the poetic and exotic qualities of the new landscape in their depictions of dramatic ice caves, glaciers and mountains shrouded in mist. A few of these visitors settled in centres such as Vancouver and Victoria, forming the core of what would be a permanent community of British Columbia artists. Living with the forests and mountains of the province, they were forced to reconcile traditional styles with the wild terrain and to explore the aesthetic possibilities of this new landscape.

Chapter 4   Maintaining a Tradition: Victoria and Vancouver 1900-25

By the turn of the century a more diversified view of the British Columbia landscape had emerged. Settlers were slowly penetrating the province's wilderness, travelling through it, clearing it, taming it. The formation of the Canadian Alpine Club, dedicated to bringing Canadians "to an appreciation of their mountain heritage," and the founding of national and provincial parks designating recreational areas, contributed to the idea that the wilderness, the "leagues upon leagues . . . [of] lonely places with no human habitation in sight," had its own aesthetic appeal.[1] One could, wrote a turn-of-the-century author, "wonder and delight at the gigantic cedar trees and the luxuriant masses of ferns."[2] However, while some British Columbians were cultivating an appreciation of the wilderness, others, especially newcomers from abroad, still appreciated only that which conformed to old-world landscape conceptions.

Travelling by rail through the Rockies in 1920, Rudyard Kipling found the British Columbia landscape foreign to the rest of Canada. The Rockies' jade lakes belonged to Tibet or some unexplored valley behind Kinchinjunga. Their Alpine valleys with "slow streams, fat pastures, and park-like uplands, with little towns, and cow bells tinkling among berry bushes"[3] were reminiscent of the landscape surrounding a Swiss hamlet. Seven years earlier Rupert Brooke had also noted the "other-worldly serenity" of the Rockies and Selkirks. "Desolation was most vividly present," he wrote, "the pines drooped and sobbed," the general landscape was "windswept and empty." To love the country here was "like embracing a wraith." For Brooke the landscape offered nothing to satisfy the hunger of a European's heart. There were no "haunted woods" or the "friendly presence of ghosts."[4] Even the more cultivated regions of Vancouver and Victoria brought no recognition of the familiar. The island capital, despite its reputation for Englishness, was foreign: "No England is set in any such seas or so fully charged with mystery of the larger ocean beyond."[5] Windswept, desolate, alien, a region scarcely blemished by man and lacking the historical associations from which the imagination could take flight, the landscape was outside the conventional comprehension of Kipling and Brooke. For them the province could only be perceived as a foreign place or a foreboding wasteland.

British Columbia's artists experienced difficulties not unlike those of Brooke and Kipling. J. Rutheford Blaikie, a member of Victoria's Vancouver Island Arts and Crafts Society, commented upon their problems. British Columbia had, he said in 1913, numerous painters who brought with them charming English studies but then "failed to produce anything approaching the same class of work from the local material." Even practised hands, strong in freshly acquired technique, full of hopeful enthusiasm for the natural beauty of the new country, were disappointing in their achievements: "Somehow they fail, one after another, to produce the results that former works seem to warrant." Blaikie analyzed the difficulties which this new wilderness, despite its scenic beauty, presented to the artists. The absence of aged and romantic associations, so disquieting to Brooke, was an artistic impediment. Artists complained that there was "nothing old, nothing of historical interest." Unable to accept this, Blaikie sought age and romance in the material at hand. "The hills and glaciers of the newest country," he insisted, "are tolerably old, and the history of the 'cleared' land and the 'railroad' is as full of human endeavor and romance as acres won by a hail of lead or a well-timed disposition of troops." The absence of ancient associations was one difficulty; the atmosphere was another. Artists complained that British Columbia's atmosphere was "too clear," with "no room for poetic graduations occasioned by mists, or even smoke."[6] Emily Carr, when sketching in England, had noted that "distance gradations were easier here to get than in our clear Canadian atmosphere and great spaces."[7] The raw wilderness and the clear atmosphere baffled the immigrant artists.

The immensity of the scenery was itself an obstacle. The terrain surrounding Vancouver was "almost unpaintable." The mountains were "too big, too proud and magnificent to come within the scope of [the] picturesque." Artists, seeking that quality, had to confine themselves "to smaller subjects with an eye to composition and effect."[8] Yet even the dogwood, aptly picturesque, was for

Thomas Bamford,
Mount Baker from Beacon Hill,
ca. 1909,
watercolour, 5-15/16 x 9-3/16.
Private Collection.

one frustrated artist "ungettable"—it was always "either buried in bushes or too high above one or something."[9]

Despite the complaint that the mountains were too huge to be paintable, they were the most popular subjects. The Olympics or Mount Baker from Victoria or the Lions from Vancouver were undeniable attractions to the artist grappling with his views. They were usually painted at sunrise or sunset when "a peculiar angle at which the rays touch the slopes or elevations render them more perceptible than at other times."[10] Early morning and evening were the best time for painting "as the colors are more in masses," the distant places more distinct, and "the soft grey tints are clearly seen."[11] In painting, Vancouver artist and teacher John Kyle prescribed that "the eyes should be half closed" in order to see tones, the relative depth of shades and the depth of colour masses. And he advised his students, "never sit in direct sunlight, unless under an umbrella."[12]

The pictures in turn-of-the-century exhibitions confirmed the clinging to older and more familiar conventions. The gallery walls of Vancouver and Victoria were crowded with depictions of Whitby Abbey, London enshrouded in fog and paintings of mist on the Cornish coast. Immigrant artists showed their English work or, like William Percival Weston, continued for years to work from Old Country sketches. Local paintings emulated British scenes as uncertain artists chose views of fruit orchards "surrounded by picturesque fences" and similar formulae.[13] The prescription for painting was representational and realistic. Nature was to be imitated. "A good picture," wrote Vancouver art columnist James Leyland, should have its "tone values correct, and atmosphere which distinctly shows the conditions under which it is painted. . . . The beholder should see the very spot indicated and be carried in imagination to it."[14]

In Victoria, the English tradition was well displayed at the Vancouver Island Arts and Crafts Society's 1910 inaugural exhibition. Landscapes far outnumbered all else, depicting outdoor scenes ranging from "dainty little local sketches to the majestic mountain and forest scenery of the Selkirks"[15]—and the inevitable Cornish coast. Most of the artists were untrained amateurs—genteel ladies, retired colonels, businessmen hobbyists. A few, like Thomas Bamford and Samuel Maclure, had received some training, and Sophie Pemberton, with study in London and Paris, was a fully finished artist.

Employed as a draughtsman with the provincial government, British-born Thomas Bamford accompanied survey parties into Vancouver Island and the mainland's wilderness. Although he captured these remote areas in his sketchbook, few were later transcribed into watercolour. Bamford preferred to render the tamer landscape in the immediate vicinity of Victoria. "Mount Baker from Beacon Hill," a view admired by Warre in 1845 and Coleman two decades later, possesses the clarity and precision of a Japanese watercolour, indicating little association with the more rugged aspects of British Columbia. Although one critic felt that "with the aid of masters" Bamford could produce much superior work, his portrayal of cultivated areas and uninhibited views were satisfactory to fellow Victorians who found his work "quite charming . . . well composed and painted."[16]

Samuel Maclure was one of the few British Columbia-born artists of his generation. Architecture, into which he poured his full creative power, was his livelihood and first love. He stamped Victoria's Rockland Heights and Vancouver's Point Grey with adaptations of the arts and crafts revival in domestic architecture. Landscape painting remained a relaxing hobby. After a course in watercolours while studying architecture at Philadelphia's Spring Garden Art School, his work evolved from the stiff realism of "Fraser River Delta" to the softness of "Olympics from Beacon Hill." Like Bamford, Maclure painted parkland scenes or views of the Olympics from Victoria's Beacon Hill, and the North Shore mountains from Vancouver's Point Grey. Had a heart condition not prevented him from venturing further into the forest and mountains, his subjects might have been more wild and diversified. Unlike most of his contemporaries he realized that "the New World required a different technique to express its individual quality"[17] and he later supported the innovative styles of both the Group of Seven and Emily Carr.

One native artist who did devote full time to her painting was

Samuel Maclure,
Fraser River Delta, 1888,
watercolour, 8½ x 12-3/16.
Private Collection.

Samuel Maclure,
Olympics from Beacon Hill,
ca. 1910,
watercolour, 4½ x 6-13/16
(sight).
Private Collection.

Sophie Pemberton,
Spring Picnic, 1902,
watercolour, 10-7/16 x
18-7/16 (sight).
Collection of Mrs. A.L.
Harvey, Victoria, B.C.

Sophie Pemberton, the daughter of Joseph Despard Pemberton, a member of the first legislature of the colony of Vancouver Island. Leaving Canada in the early 1890s, Sophie Pemberton began a career which won her distinction at the South Kensington School, the Académie Julian, and praise at the Paris Salon and the Royal Academy. Londoners admired the "high-pitched colors" of her British Columbia landscapes. The "delight in the golden-yellows and darkling purples and ultra-deep-marine hues and vivid greens" in "Spring Picnic," was characteristic, they felt, of the scenery of Vancouver Island's "demi-England."[18] Yet Victoria critics found the vibrant colour of her Vancouver Island landscapes too harsh, preferring the muted colour and charm of her French oils. Like Emily Carr, Pemberton realized, especially after returning from England, that British Columbia required a different portrayal. She sought to do this in the brilliant greens, purples and yellows of her landscape paintings. British Columbians, however, were generally unprepared for any deviation from the English landscape tradition.

Maude Lettice, Margaret Kitto and Josephine Crease were among the many genteel ladies of Victoria's Island Arts and Crafts Society who had been trained locally and for whom painting, although taken seriously, was largely a social activity. They organized sketching parties, they served tea at the annual exhibitions and were among the staunchest guardians of the realist tradition. "On the Mountain Side, Saanich Arm" is typical, in quality and subject matter, of the tradition they sought to preserve. Although Maude Lettice is in the forest she has chosen a spot where the trees do not engulf, the underbrush does not choke and the sun penetrates the forest floor with ease. The gently rising mist mutes the dark forest, the sloping hills intersected by the conifers give the painting all the conventionalities of a view piece. While there is little suggestion here of the true British Columbia forest, there is much reminiscent of how early twentieth-century artists in Victoria chose to view it.

In Vancouver, where "the quest of the dollar . . . [left] no time for the quest of the beautiful," there was a "lack of sympathetic atmosphere, lack of encouragement" for the "gallant little band" of artists.[19] Turn-of-the-century Vancouver had, however, a larger number of professionally trained artists who selflessly devoted as much time to art education and the promotion of the arts, as to their own painting. For the most part their landscape paintings were a product of their South Kensington, Slade or Royal Academy training. W.P. Weston was so wedded to the English landscape that he worked exclusively from English sketches and picture postcards during his first years in Vancouver. Other immigrant British artists turned directly to the local landscape, but the results, as Blaikie pointed out, did not reflect the quality of their former work. However, Grace Judge found a convention outside of the English landscape tradition to soften and humanize the landscape. She employed the decorative style of Arthur Rackham and Edmond Dulac. A style suited to a fairy-tale landscape would hardly seem appropriate for the British Columbia forest. And yet in "The Old House, Roberts Creek," the forest has been wonderfully adapted and appears distinctively British Columbian.

The English realist tradition was most successfully adapted to the British Columbia landscape by Thomas Fripp, whose education in the British school of Cox, de Wint and Cotman, at St. John's Wood Art School and the Royal Academy was completed with a year of study in Italy. Although trained to follow the careers of his well-known watercolourist father, George Arthur Fripp, and uncle, Alfred Fripp, when he arrived in British Columbia in 1893, Thomas

Maude Lettice,
*On the Mountain Side, Saanich
Arm*, ca. 1910,
watercolour, 12¼ x 9.
Private Collection.

Grace Judge,
*The Old House, Roberts Creek,
B.C.*, 1919,
watercolour, 18½ x 14½.
Private Collection.

did not paint. He homesteaded at Hatzic until an injury incurred while clearing land forced him to abandon farming and resume his artistic career. Selling his farm, he moved to a half-acre site overlooking the Fraser River and rented a small studio on Pender Street in Vancouver. Now dependent upon art for his livelihood and devoting his full attention to it, Fripp fully explored British Columbia's mountainous regions. The summers found him sketching on the Cheakamus River with his son Humphrey, at Alta Lake with his daughter Jo and on the glaciers in Jasper Park with summer students. In the winter he taught in his Vancouver studio and devoted much time and energy to promoting artistic development. A member and variously president of the Art, Historical and Scientific Association, the Sketch Club, the Palette and Chisel Club, the British Columbia Society of Fine Arts and the Art League, Fripp probably did "more for the cause of art in Vancouver than any

Thomas Fripp,
Mount Omega, Tantalus Range,
1925,
watercolour, 14½ x 21.
The Vancouver Art Gallery.

other one man."[20] At the same time he demonstrated that a Vancouver artist could survive, however modestly, upon his art alone.

Unlike many of his contemporaries, Fripp understood the distinction between the primitive wilderness of British Columbia and the romantic antiquity of his native England. British Columbia possessed "no picturesque chalets, no castles or ancient architecture"; here was only "pure wild nature." To soften the "wilderness and primitive savagery,"[21] to heighten the atmospheric effects and complement the harmonies of his pictures, he painted in grey weather, at twilight, or in the misty morning. "Mount Omega, Tantalus Range" is a superb example of the dramatic nuances he sought to achieve. In the upper regions of the earth he found the "poetic graduations" of mists and clouds which less observant artists complained the atmosphere lacked.[22]

Fripp's mountain mists, so characteristic of the coastal ranges, sometimes tend to veil the landscape's more rugged features. Yet solidity and massiveness remain. The mountain and foreground boulder of "With the Dying Sun" convey the feeling of solidity and

Thomas Fripp,
With the Dying Sun, 1919,
watercolour, 27½ x 18⅞.
Vancouver City Archives.

surface[23] for which his father's Alpine pictures were famous. Fripp's trees, however, are weightless, lacking the mass which welds the mountain and boulder to the earth. The "vast forests that fill the valleys and clothe the lower slopes" offered no challenge. It was only when he passed to "the glaciers and their snow-clad peaks towering above" that Fripp met with the feeling of "defiance and resentment."[24] In "Mount Omega" he concentrated on the peak where the ultimate defiance of the mountain could be manifested without the distraction of foreground trees. Everything is subservient to the mountain. Even the mists are translucent, leaving the mountain's form unobstructed while creating an impression of illimitable heights. The peak lunges forward, the sole commanding force in the painting.

Fripp was traditional and romantic, yet he did have something of the "fresh vision" he felt British Columbia landscape art needed.[25] It is true, as W.J. Phillips noted, that "progressive thought passed him by."[26] With no others to discuss his problems, with no paintings to study, to admire, emulate or revile, his artistic ideals remained those that had thrived in St. John's Wood in his youth.

Painting on into an age when Jock Macdonald, F.H. Varley and Charles Scott were working with new ideas and forms, he cheered at their setbacks. Untouched by "modernism," he remained the touchstone of "sanity" in British Columbia art, although a 1909 reviewer already thought his paintings "too pretty."[27]

Fripp attempted to overcome the problems of subject matter and atmosphere. By focusing on mountain peaks under the graduated atmosphere of vapour and cloud, he gave them poetic and ageless grandeur. His contemporaries were rarely so successful. They contrived their subject matter from picturesque preconceptions or resorted to the artificialities of sunset colours. They relied on hilltop views, never penetrating to the forest depths or mountain peaks. The forest remained alien—monotonous as a green smear on a slope where the sun could not "penetrate into the forest gloom."[28] For the most part the British Columbia artists of the early twentieth century could not accept their landscape on its own terms. They could not go into it, feel it, hear it. Most remained caught in the withering and anachronistic English tradition with its emphasis on realism and atmosphere. They failed to see that in British Columbia those twin goals were often contradictory. Oddly, the artists were rather self-satisfied with their efforts. They were proud of their isolation and independence, of their avoidance both of modern "shell-shocked productions"[29] and of mere transcriptions of European subjects or Canadian scenes painted in a European manner. To their admirers they were a group of artists who were committed to "a sincere study and understanding of nature in the glorious elemental and unusual forms in which she presents her beauties in British Columbia."[30] But the complacency would not last. Although the majority of early twentieth-century artists in British Columbia were producing works that largely derived from old-world traditions, a few, led by individuals like C.J. Collings and Statira Frame, were beginning to grasp the notion "that a picture may fulfil another mission than being a mere accurate representation of physical fact."[31]

Chapter 5   Divergences: C. J. Collings, W. J. Phillips and Statira Frame

While Thomas Fripp's watercolours may have been out-of-date by the early 1920s, they represented for the isolated Vancouver art community the ideal of landscape art during the first two and a half decades of the century. Realistic, yet tinged with romantic effects, Fripp's painting set a standard of approach and technique which other artists tried to emulate. Any departure from this style would be scorned since it was important for the burgeoning art communities of British Columbia to maintain consistent artistic standards. While this demand for aesthetic conformity enabled artists to set common standards for the schools, galleries and advisory boards that were the backbone of a strong art community, such rigid ideals could also become dangerously static and ingrown. As one reviewer put it: "One of the great dangers to which any small and select artistic society is always exposed is the danger of becoming a church ... the infusion of any new doctrine is quite naturally regarded as heresy."[1]

A number of artists emerged after 1910 who, in the eyes of many adherents to the traditional landscape style, abandoned their artistic principles. Departing from standards they found obsolete, Statira Frame, Margaret Wake, Harry Hood and Ann Batchelor drew their inspiration from modern French schools of painting. Charles John Collings combined the best of English decorative and traditional Japanese watercolour styles. Emphasis shifted from mountain and panorama views to the more intimate aspects of the landscape—the curve of a glacier, a forest clearing or a summer cottage amid tangled woods. Their British Columbia landscape was not clearly and faithfully delineated, but expressed in opaque pools of wash or gay dabs of oil. These artists interpreted rather than realistically portrayed what they saw.

In 1912 when Charles John Collings exhibited his paintings of the uninhabited regions of the Rockies and Shuswap Lake at the Carroll Gallery in London, he took British art circles by surprise. His work was hailed as one of the most remarkable achievements since the days of Turner.[2] Not only did his paintings recall some of Turner's Rhineland sketches, but they possessed a feeling for design and colour found in the best work of Hiroshige. Subtlely blending English and Japanese schools, Collings offered a new perception of the dramatic aspects of the Rockies and Selkirks.

Collings' beginnings in his native Devon were modest. His early ambition to become an architect was diverted by his family's inability to finance his schooling. He apprenticed to a county solicitor and for twenty years copied legal documents, until later financial success at various enterprises gave him the freedom to pursue art more seriously. He took a few lessons from the animal painter N.H.J. Baird, met Frank Brangwyn by whom he was influenced, and exhibited, not without praise, at the Royal Academy. In 1903 he achieved some fame with a one-man show at the Dowdeswell Gallery in London, where critics compared his paintings with those of Turner. Not liking the comparison, Collings remained "quiescent, painting but little, and—with the exception of 'one-man shows'—refusing to send his productions to any Exhi-

Charles John Collings, *Nearing the Glacier,* no date, watercolour, 5⅛ x 7⅛ (sight). Maltwood Memorial Museum of Historic Art, University of Victoria, B.C.

Charles John Collings, *Mountain Stream in Winter,* no date, watercolour, 5¼ x 7¼ (sight). Maltwood Memorial Museum of Historic Art, University of Victoria, B.C.

bition whatever." According to his cousin and promoter, Luscombe Carroll, it was this incident which determined his "self-chosen exile," at sixty, to the new orchard settlement on Shuswap Lake.[3]

A member of the English Alpine Club, Collings was an ardent climber. High in the Rockies and Selkirks he ignored the views of mountain gorges and peaks which had been Fripp's challenge. Instead, his vigorous and direct sketches embraced the insignificant facts of the landscape—a rock face, a hillside, the gentle twist of a glacial stream. Transcribed into watercolours, "Nearing the Glacier" has no textbook perspective, no sense of space, height, mass or distance and no meticulous detail. By applying only a few colours Collings created an ambience revealing that there is "much behind and beyond the ordinary vision, not expressed by abstractions, but by color and form related to nature."[4]

The success of such watercolours lay partly in Collings' method of execution. He soaked a sheet of hot-pressed paper in water for a day or two and, when ready to paint, laid it on a sheet of glass or cork to preserve the moisture. Using pure pigments of full intensity, he mixed the colours directly on the paper. Muddiness never resulted. Where the masses of floating colour met, they combined into forms and hues of great beauty. The method gave Collings' imagination free rein, although he did work from a fairly detailed sketch methodically inscribed with colour notations and light effects. Having this plan before him, he was not hampered by the masses of detail which often distract an artist and was able to work quickly, producing what one critic described as "little lyrics in paint."[5]

Collings' success at the Carroll Gallery in 1912 was largely attributed, by London critics, to his presence in the British Columbia landscape. "His wild surroundings," wrote one critic, "ministered to the needs of his brush" and "helped to determine his final method of expression."[6] Another claimed that "such an experience and long sojourn far from the restless confusion of modern life have given him . . . an Olympian detachment."[7] That Collings developed his "mystical understanding of the Earth Force"[8] in the Rockies seemed no surprise. In fact, critics said, it was "the wide spaces and the dramatic aspects of Nature in British Columbia" that "played a part in creating the serenity of his vision and the peculiar quality of his sense of pictorial form."[9]

No doubt Collings' pioneer life on Shuswap Lake, especially during the chilling winters, would have taught him something about the elements. The natural beauty of his surroundings was unquestionably inspiring. English landscape painting could, as Emily Carr wrote, be "indolent seeing, ready-made compositions, needing only to be copied."[10] Yet the new landscape, as other immigrants could testify, was not easy to capture. Fripp had stressed the necessity of a period of contemplation before one could successfully translate the landscape into paint. Collings had to struggle; it took time and study before he could satisfactorily draw the conifers around him.[11] But although Collings' style changed in British Columbia, his 1903 Dowdeswell Galleries pictures had already possessed the qualities that marked his mature Canadian work.[12] The same instinct for decorative pattern, the same rare sense of colour (though not opacity), the same very distinctive technique was evident in his earlier works. Life in the mountains gave Collings the leisure to develop those qualities. That he had an "Olympian detachment" is certain. He rarely exhibited with the Vancouver and Victoria art societies, sold largely through the Carroll Gallery in London and, according to his son Guy, had no British Columbia artist friends. Apart from a trip to England in 1920 Collings remained relatively unaware of artistic trends in London or British Columbia. His fine collection of oriental paintings and woodcuts hint that his subtle ideas of colour may have been drawn from the early Japanese masters. What the Rockies gave him (and this would have been true had he retired to some hamlet in England's lake district) was the solitude to develop a singular perception of the landscape without the interference of critics or the influence of other artists.

Like Collings, Walter J. Phillips revealed in his work a gentle, contemplative attitude toward nature. Born and trained in Britain, Phillips grew up within the tradition of English landscape painting. "The beauty and wonders of Nature are as alluring as the pursuit of Art," he wrote, "and made of me a landscape painter."[13] Coming to Winnipeg in 1913, he initially made the prairies and lakes his sketching grounds, but in the late 1920s he turned increasingly to

Walter J. Phillips,
*Vapours Round the Mountain
Curled,* 1938,
colour woodcut, 8-13/16 x
10-15/16.
Private Collection.

mountain scenes and West Coast Indian themes, producing a series
of exquisitely drawn pictures and perfectly executed colour wood-
cuts.

Phillips discovered that the "virgin country or the forest
primeval" did not stimulate his imagination "so certainly as that
in which the hand of man is apparent."[14] Canada's wilderness was
to him unfriendly, remote from the haunts of men, unsuggestive
of the comfort of human meaning. Yet he, like Collings, demonstrated that this traditional perception of nature need not be inap-
propriate to Canadian landscape. When painting in the Rockies or
on the West Coast, he portrayed vistas with dramatic clarity and
quiet awe. As often, however, he found beauty in landscape that
was intensified by human contrast—the picturesque simplicity of
a wharf against the sea and mountains or the stark beauty of Indian
totems in their forest setting. In the intimacy of a waterfall or a
wildflower he found a simple beauty that was "balm to the soul."[15]
The emphasis was always upon the tranquil, upon the "better

Walter J. Phillips,
Howe Sound, B.C., 1935,
colour woodcut, 10½ x 12⅞.
Private Collection.

beauty" to be discovered while nature was in repose.[16] Remarkably sensitive to atmosphere, colour, variation and form, Phillips drew from the British Columbia landscape an expression that revealed a passionate, "almost pagan" love of nature.[17] Although decorative and realistic, Phillips' works never merely transcribe the literal. The painter, he wrote, "rends the veil of appearance and discloses significant and fundamental truths which he incorporates in his designs; such things as the rhythm of growth, the essence and interrelation of form, the interdependence of all things, the essential solidity of rock and the tenuity of vapour."[18]

Called by the Society of Fine Arts British Columbia's "pioneer in modernism,"[19] Statira Frame departed from the English landscape tradition by taking her inspiration from the French Post-Impressionists. Unlike Collings and Phillips, she did not venture into the mountains; Vancouver's Stanley Park, the north arm of Burrard Inlet, the Fraser Valley, Victoria and Alert Bay comprise the extent of her wanderings throughout the province.

When Quebec-born Statira Frame arrived in British Columbia in 1892, she could not boast of having hung in the Royal Academy or of having studied in any of the Paris ateliers from where she drew her inspiration. Except for a term in clay-modelling at the Vancouver Night School, she never took lessons. Frame was put on the Post-Impressionist track by Emily Carr who, upon returning from study in France, lived with the Frame family for several weeks. It was not until Frame was well into her artistic career that she received the helpful criticism of Robert Henri and Arnim Hansen. New York artist and teacher Robert Henri received four of Statira Frame's oil sketches for "crits" in the winter of 1917, and advised her to "go on." In a lengthy critique of her work, Henri provided Frame with the enthusiasm and confidence she needed. He saw in her work "an interest in the beautiful design of nature—a very decided sensitiveness to the orchestration of color, [and a] good sense of form." She sensed beauty and romance, he felt, in the reality of nature. Of her colour he was certain: "I think you see color in beautiful order in nature. You see color in construction— some people only see color and more color. The great thing is *what happens between colors.*" Henri warned Frame not to take lessons, but to educate herself by watching "the voice that comes from within you ... not an outside educated voice." If Frame would follow, not coddle, her respect for nature, her sense of colour and composition and her originality would blossom.[20]

A visit to San Francisco around 1921 gave Statira Frame another stimulus—introduction to the Post-Impressionist work of Arnim Hansen. Although largely a painter of marine subjects, the "lusty masculine vigor" of his non-photographic work prompted Frame to seek him out. Finding Hansen at his Pacific Street stable-studio in Monterey, she persuaded him to give her "crits." Although there is no record of how Hansen taught Frame, one student recalled that the best thing about his classes was that he had no set theories or systems. Placing a large canvas in front of a student, he advised two things: "see color and use lots of paint."[21] Statira Frame must have followed his advice; her colours became more vibrant and she turned to a larger sixteen-by-twenty-inch format.

Robert Henri noted that Statira Frame's strength lay in her ability to translate colour and sunlight to the canvas. F.H. Varley once remarked that he would give a lot to have her "fine sense of color."[22] Working out-of-doors, generally in oils, Frame blotted out details with broad strokes and patches of colour. She favoured leaf-greens, purples and pinks, yet never allowed one to upset the orchestration of the others. Her compositions were often characterized by a diagonal stream, road or object intersecting the canvas.

Uninhibited by the academicism that was sometimes too apparent in the works of Thomas Fripp, Statira Frame painted with a spontaneity that gave freshness to the Vancouver art scene. "As adventures in color and composition," wrote one reviewer, "her paintings have introduced a new and refreshing note in all the exhibitions in which they have been shown."[23] The more conservative patrons, about whom Emily Carr had occasion to complain in her autobiography,[24] were not so convinced of Statira Frame's vision. One felt that the work lacked atmosphere and perspective, that she only imagined what she saw.[25] Another wrote of her "crude strength of handling" and her sense of colour which prompted her "occasionally to renounce correct drawing for larger masses and contrasts."[26] But generally, as was the case with Carr, she was patiently tolerated as a "daring colorist."[27] No doubt Henri's praise gave credibility to a style about which the conservative element of the community felt uneasy. Rarely was the name of Frame mentioned in the 1920s without reference to the commendation by the New York artist and critic.

While Statira Frame was undoubtedly British Columbia's "pioneer in modernism," Margaret Wake, Ann Batchelor, Harry Hood and Mary Riter Hamilton illustrated that she was not the only artist to be influenced by modern movements from abroad. Arriving in Vancouver from their native England in 1911, Margaret Wake and Ann Batchelor taught at the Studio Club 17 on Hastings Street before sharing a West End apartment and studio. Although Margaret Wake's work initially demonstrated the conventionality of her Slade School background, it gradually became freer, bolder and less structured. By 1925 a local reviewer felt that she was not showing her "usual masterly style" and in 1928 another noted that

◄ Statira Frame,
Cottage on Burrard Inlet, 1922,
oil on board, 12-9/16 x 18.
Private Collection.

Margaret Wake,　►
Path to the Seven Sisters, no date,
watercolour, 13½ x 9½ (sight).
Private Collection.

◄ Harry Hood,
Thunderstorm, Burrard Inlet,
B.C., ca. 1925,
oil on board, 9¼ x 12⅛.
Private Collection.

a portrait had "many good qualities, but eyes are the windows to the soul and usually have pupils, none are shown in this portrait."[28] Her leaning toward the modern school was evident in landscape as well as portraiture. Summer excursions to Savary Island where she and Batchelor had rented a cottage, and short sketching trips

to Stanley Park gave Wake much opportunity to interpret the landscape. "Path to the Seven Sisters" evinces the radical departure from the meticulous watercolours of her former work. Wake's painting is loose yet controlled. The patches of colour evoke an immensely pleasing feeling of cool shade and warm pools of sunlight rather than articulating the precise details of the spot where the scene was captured.

Mary Riter Hamilton and Harry Hood were no less ignorant of new movements. Ontario-born Mary Riter Hamilton had eight years of study in Paris behind her when she arrived in Victoria in about 1912. Although she generally reworked many of her European paintings, catering to Victoria and Vancouver's art societies' taste, she did occasionally turn to the British Columbia landscape for inspiration. Her work, known to reviewers as "convincing and broadly-painted,"[29] did not approach the freeness or liberal use of colour in the works of Frame or Wake.

Scottish-born Harry Hood had studied drawing and design at the South Kensington School of Art. However, when he came to Vancouver in 1904 he earned his living as a piano tuner. Although he continued painting, it was not until he acquired the Art Emporium in 1926 that he was brought fully into the artistic scene. During those years under Hood's proprietorship the Art Emporium became a centre for British Columbia's "avant-garde." Like Batchelor and Wake, his early British Columbia work was traditional. From the late twenties, however, he demonstrated an inclination toward French Impressionism. "Thunderstorm over Burrard Inlet" is a superb rendering of the light and cloud effects over sea and mountains.

The British Columbia artists of the early 1900s who deviated from the traditional English landscape style had little impact on the rest of the Vancouver and Victoria art communities. Collings and Wake rarely exhibited their landscapes; Hood did not "turn modern" until the end of the twenties and Frame was a tolerated exception. None held influential positions in art schools or on art advisory boards. They were, however, symptomatic of new movements which would affect the style of painting and the perception of the landscape in the following decades.

Chapter 6   The Erosion of Isolation: Contacts and Influences 1920-30

The railway connection between British Columbia and central Canada that had been completed in 1885 deprived the province of its western isolation, attaching it tenuously by a thin band of steel to the rest of the Dominion. The tourist artists who travelled that line in the last years of the nineteenth century had, however, little permanent impact upon the art of the province or upon the developing landscape perception of British Columbians. Despite the visitors from Europe and central Canada and the short Parisian experiences of Sophie Pemberton and Emily Carr, the artistic influences upon the cultural life of the small communities remained preponderantly British. Immigrant Britons like Thomas Fripp and Grace Judge had set landscape standards that tended to be traditional and conservative. These standards partly reflected the outlook of a colonial and provincial immigrant community, cut off from the developments of the country's metropolitan centres and as yet without a dynamic centre of its own. As much, however, they were a consequence of the traditionalism of British art itself, tardy in awakening to the developments of continental art, of French Impressionism and northern European Expressionism.

After World War I the isolationism of British Columbia was eroded at an ever-increasing rate and the province began to pull away from its traditional ideals of realism. That view had outlived its age, had reached its apotheosis in the marvellous romantic realism of Thomas Fripp and his imitators. The perception of the landscape and its artistic representation now began to change. External detail was increasingly neglected as artists searched for structure and form, for essence and spirit.

The struggle against the disadvantage of distance was persistent and fruitful. An increasing number of art exhibitions came to the province. The fall fairs in New Westminster, Vancouver and Victoria provided the greatest exposure and from 1916 the National Gallery, which was beginning to take an interest in the West, loaned pictures to the annual exhibitions as well as to facilities provided by the British Columbia Art League of Vancouver and the Island Arts and Crafts Society of Victoria. The Pacific Northwest exhibitions in Seattle attracted an increasing number of British Columbians, putting provincial artists in touch with a neighbouring region that was emerging as a vital artistic centre. A few British Columbians began sending pictures to central Canadian shows as well.

In 1925 a group of leading businessmen made their initial offer of financial assistance toward a permanent civic gallery, a move that eventuated in the opening of the Vancouver Art Gallery six years later. In the same period, John Vanderpant, perhaps the greatest Canadian photographer of his time, was operating a gallery on Robson Street which became an informal centre for advanced ideas in art and music. Harry Täuber, one of the chief exponents of Vienna's Expressionist theatre of the 1920s and avant-garde European movements, settled in Vancouver, bringing with him an enthusiasm for expressionism, constructivism and spiritualism. The greatest agent for the departure from insularity, however, was the newly established Vancouver School of Applied and Decorative Art.

The founding of the Vancouver School was the result of long effort by the art community of the city. At last established in 1925 under the auspices of the city school board, the principalship fell to Charles H. Scott, an Ayrshireman trained in Glasgow who had settled in Vancouver in 1912 as art supervisor in the school system. For the full-time faculty of the new school Scott recruited Grace Melvin, also a product of the Glasgow School; J.W.G. (Jock) Macdonald, a commercial designer and a graduate of the Edinburgh School; and Frederick Horsman Varley, one of the leading members of the Ontario Group of Seven.

The mid-1920s, moreover, saw an increasing number of artists who came from outside the province to paint British Columbia's scenery. Foreign visitors were few, although the American, John Singer Sargent, was in the Rockies briefly in 1916 and the Australian, Arthur Streeton, painted for weeks in Victoria and the Rockies in 1923. But much more important was the Group of Seven.

This school of painters had already affected a revolution in taste in Ontario and Quebec landscape painting by their preference for the rugged terrain of the Laurentian Shield. In the mid-1920s four of them turned their attentions to the far West. A.Y. Jackson, who had briefly been to the Jasper region in 1914, returned ten years later, this time with Lawren Harris. J.E.H. MacDonald visited Lake O'Hara that same summer and found the area so irresistable that he returned annually until 1930. Harris also caught Rocky Mountain fever, painting there for four consecutive summers. Arthur Lismer, another of the Group, went west for the first time in 1928. The Indian communities of British Columbia also attracted Jackson and Edwin Holgate.

Many of these Group of Seven painters were, at least initially, very much like their summer-season predecessors. J.E.H. MacDonald's first visit had all the exoticism of hiring a cowboy guide, of discovering larch trees, marmots and an August snowfall.[1] The Toronto critic, Barker Fairley, singled out this weakness in the Group's first Rocky Mountain season. Art, Fairley insisted, was a different thing from travel and scenery; an artist must know nature before using her: "Just when the Group is beginning to know the North better, and to gain mastery of it, off they go West to a country which none of them have in their bones."[2] The Group, however, while essentially central Canadian, refused to consider any part of Canada to be outside their range. They exalted in their expansiveness, aiming at making the whole of Canada a sketching ground. Although Jackson never warmed to the mountains—they were, he said, "not my line"[3]—he found other portions of the province, such as the Skeena and Cariboo regions, more paintable. MacDonald's struggles with the Rockies finally met with success when he lowered his sights from the peaks to the bases. Lismer's monumental "Cathedral Mountain" invests that giant with a craggy, petrified solidity. Harris was by the late twenties well on his way toward cosmic abstraction and his mountains are serious essays in stylizing the landscape into an essential form, searching for a spirituality in the mountain ranges that his friend F.B. Housser considered to be "sacred and occult centres of the earth."[4]

More important than the Group's local pictures, however, was the vigour of the perception which they brought to the Canadian landscape. They cast aside the pastoral and the picturesque, seeking in the rough, raw wilderness a new kind of beauty and a moral and spiritual meaning. Choosing Canada's "raw youthful homeliness" instead of the "traditional pastoral quality of the older countries," the Group celebrated the virtue of wilderness.[5] They largely passed over areas where man's presence could be seen in favour of discovering the "real" Canada. In Lismer's eyes Canada was "rugged and stern over large areas, untamed—perhaps untamable," a place "for the elemental forces of nature to sport in."[6]

Emphasizing the wild and savage in the landscape, the Group almost entirely suppressed the human presence. Their land was solitary, empty and silent. Man, dwarfed into insignificance by elemental nature, "has no governance here."[7] Yet the land had a spiritual meaning for the observer. It humbled him by its physical presence and permeated him with its spiritual force. There were "cosmic powers behind the bleakness and barrenness and austerity of much of the land," and for man, "a consciousness of harmony in the universe, the perception of the divine order running through all existence."[8]

To a man of W.J. Phillips' quiet sensitivity, this emphasis upon the wilderness was a dwelling upon the repellent and inhospitable.

A.Y. Jackson,
Mt. Gitsegyukla, Upper Skeena,
1926,
pencil, 7¾ x 9½.
The McMichael Canadian
Collection, Kleinburg,
Ontario.

The Group dealt, he wrote, "almost exclusively with the less pleasing aspects of our country."[9] Their wilderness ethos, however, was not an artistic aberration, but very much a reflection of a decisive shift in taste.

The Group's passion for the wilderness was closely associated with the rapid urban growth which had put the city resident out of daily contact with nature. The resultant back-to-nature movement expressed itself in the expanded use of wilderness parks such as Algonquin, and the increased popularity of summer camps and lakeside cottages. Paralleling a similar trend in the United States,[10] the wilderness movement provided a new conception of nature and of Canadians' relationship to it.

In a sense the wilderness ethos was a return to the eighteenth-

Lawren Harris,
Mount Lefroy, 1930,
oil on canvas, 57¼ x 60⅜.
The McMichael Canadian
Collection, Kleinburg,
Ontario.

century sublime. The Group emphasized the vastness and power of nature, were sensitive to solemnity and solitude, and depicted rugged rock, tortured pines and rushing water. Discovering the moral virtues of nature through Emerson, Thoreau, Whitman and theosophy,[11] their perception possessed the same spiritual depth as that of the eighteenth century and thus revitalized the sensitivity to nature's power that had been lost in Victorian cant. The wilderness aesthetic was particularly appropriate to British Columbia where the landscape more than matched Ontario in its wildness and immediacy.

In British Columbia, urban pressures—"these modern days of ever-increasing speed, of jazz, and of jaded nerves"—brought a desire for "the healing quiet of the out-doors."[12] Wilderness parks were established at Strathcona in 1911 and, in the next decade, in the Garibaldi area. Something of the wilderness idea had already been carefully preserved in Vancouver's Stanley Park where untrammeled nature coexisted with carefully groomed formal gardens. Victoria's Mount Douglas and Goldstream parks offered similar easily accessible areas of primeval forest. Cottaging never developed to the same extent as in Ontario, although summer homes on the waterfront of upper Burrard Inlet were popular as early as 1908. Mountaineering and camping, or just walking and picnicking, increased rapidly in the twentieth century. Garibaldi Park became a special sanctuary of the "wild and primitive" where man might "recapture that old sense of wonder in the mystery and miracle of the wilderness."[13] There he was "away from the paved and noisy streets, away from the envy and greed and pride of crowded ways."[14]

By 1925 British Columbia artists themselves were responding to the wilderness aesthetic that had been pioneered by members of Ontario's Group of Seven. Early exhibitions in 1919 and 1922 of the Group of Seven's pictures passed without much comment, but in 1928 a loan exhibition touched off a newspaper storm that brought a number of artists to the defence of the Group's aims. Young artists like Max Maynard were strongly impressed by the pictures and devoured the ideas expressed in writings by and about the Ontarians. Emily Carr, seeing the Group's pictures in 1927, felt a renewed inspiration to paint her own West. And a year earlier, the Group had been brought to Vancouver in the person of F.H. Varley at the art school.

A new generation of painters dominated Vancouver art for more than two decades after 1926. Diverse in origin, they nevertheless possessed a similar landscape perception and painting style. Charles Scott adapted his Scottish academic style to the new national and international currents of inter-war art. Varley evolved as a landscapist during his ten years in the province, while Jock Macdonald, Paul Rand and W.P. Weston developed or refined a landscape style in British Columbia which was consistent with the wilderness perception. Significant as were all of these, however, it was Emily Carr who most strikingly revealed the new perception of British Columbia's landscape.

Chapter 7   The First Conscious Expression of the Rhythm of Life: Emily Carr

With her unique interpretations of the Pacific coast's rain forest, Emily Carr strongly influenced the way in which artists and residents viewed the landscape in British Columbia. She shamelessly plunged her viewer into the wood interior, drawing patterns and rhythms out of the jungle chaos. One could no longer ignore those dark forest smears on the mountainside or struggle through the dense underbrush without pausing within its midst. After Carr, the forest was no longer considered to be gloomy, but was pulsating with the "rhythm of life."[1]

In spite of the revolutionary vision she eventually brought to British Columbia's landscape art, Carr's earliest association with the province's landscape was typical of the newly settled English community of the 1870s. Apart from family outings to Millstream, where "we could not have squeezed into the woods had we tried because they were so thick," Carr's childhood contact with the wilderness did not extend beyond the ten-acre lot that her father had made "as meek and English as he could," or the semi-wild Beacon Hill Park on which it bordered. Carr recalled being excited at hearing about her father's ten-day voyage around Vancouver Island. He brought back descriptions of "the magnificent trees, of their closeness to each other, of the strangling undergrowth, [and of] the great silence."[2] But her own journal of a bicycle excursion through the primeval forest sixteen years later records no such fascination with the wilderness. The "sombre" trees, fear of panther, bear and snake prohibited any aesthetic contemplation. She avoided the forest on this early excursion to Cowichan Lake; her sketches hugged the stream's edge and the clearing around the inn.[3]

Artistic training under Victoria's art teachers Miss Emily Woods and Miss Withrow, as well as Carr's two-and-a-half-year study at San Francisco's California School of Design, was largely confined to portraying plaster casts and still life. Only during her second San Francisco year, in L.P. Latimer's landscape class, was she introduced to painting out-of-doors. Her work took "a definite list toward pure landscape" five years later when she travelled to the remote Toxis Mission near the West Coast village of Ucluelet. But while "the lovely, wild vastness," the "one continual shove of growing" overwhelmed her, she preferred to portray the Indians and their houses: "No artist that I knew, no Art School had taught Art this size."[4] The forest of her "Indian Village," therefore, remained a silhouette behind the Indian houses.

Ironically, it was the woods of England that first inspired her to paint within the forest. Filthy, immense, over-populated London drove Carr to the St. Ives art colony in Cornwall after two years at London's Westminster School of Art. She spent the 1901-2 term at the Porthmeor studio of seascape painter Julius Olsson. There she met Algernon Talmage, a *plein air* landscape painter praised for his "highness of key and subtle diffusion of light."[5] He encouraged her discovery of the haunting, ivy-draped Tregenna Woods high above St. Ives harbour. Later, attending the Meadow Studios of John Whiteley in Bushey, Carr learned more about trees; that "the coming and going of foliage is more than just flat pattern."[6] Her work became so much a part of the English land-scape tradition that she regretted not being able to bring back a Cornish cottage and English thrushes when she returned to Canada in 1904.[7]

Back in British Columbia Carr still did not paint the forest, but like her contemporaries she exhibited an array of subjects: portraits, flower studies and landscape views as well as Indian villages. It was not until 1908 that she could be found "submerged beneath a drown of undergrowth" in Stanley Park's forest, portray-ing, on a larger format, the giant conifers.[8] But she was unsuccessful in transferring the mystery of Tregenna Wood to the British Columbia forest. Her "Wood Interior" is highly detailed, unspon-taneous and stiff. Aware that such work was little in advance of her Vancouver contemporaries and aware that British Columbia required something different for its expression, she set out in the summer of 1910 for Paris. There she hoped to learn something of the advanced French school of painting.

It was not long before Carr became stifled by the hot and stuffy classrooms of the Académie Colarossi in Paris and escaped to Brit-tany and Ile-de-France. Under the guidance of Fauve artist Henry William Phelan Gibb, whom she accompanied to Crécy-en-Brie and St. Efflam, she turned from watercolour to oil, brightened her palette, broadened and shortened her brush strokes. Later in Concarneau with New Zealand expatriate Frances Hodgkins, she returned to watercolour, toned down her palette and allowed a solid line to enclose the forms. In France she learned that there was much beyond the surface reality of painting. She was awakened to the value of light in colour and returned to Vancouver anxious to apply her new Post-Impressionist technique to the British Columbia landscape.

Carr's native landscape, however, still puzzled her. She remained "mystified, baffled as to how to tackle our big West."[9] She had difficulty in transferring Fauve and Post-Impressionist concepts to the dark green of the landscape and the bleached cedar of the Indian villages. Lacking the stimulus to continue her experi-mentation and seeking a purpose for her art, Carr poured her energy into recording the fast-disappearing totem poles and community houses of northern Indian villages. Her newly acquired Post-Impressionist and Fauve style quickly eroded. Anthropological accuracy overruled freeness of expression. The forest, for the most part, faded into a silhouetted backdrop for the totems and villages. Within a year after returning from France she was spending more time running her Victoria apartment-boarding house, "The House of All Sorts," than painting.

It was not until later that Carr renewed her interest in the British Columbia landscape itself. Viola and Ambrose Patterson were partially responsible. The Seattle artist-couple spent many weekends in the early twenties in The House of All Sorts. They found Carr starved for contact and eager to talk painting.[10] Although Paris-trained like Carr, they were attempting to find a unique way to interpret their Pacific North West landscape by brushing aside former values and deriving inspiration from the land itself. They drew Emily Carr into their circle, introducing her to other Seattle artists, inviting her to exhibit and judge at Seattle's annual Pacific North West Artists Exhibition. They also prompted her to buy Jan Gordon's *Modern French Painters* where she read of Paul Cézanne's condemnation of the picturesque as "the most dangerous of subject-matter" because it contained associations "which tend to veil by means of sentiment any shortcomings from real plastic beauty."[11]

Carr did much experimenting throughout the 1920s, perhaps following Cézanne's dicta that art was to be judged by the depth of experiment attempted in it. The few surviving paintings from this period show that she broke into a simpler, less contrived way of expressing nature. In "Deciduous Forest" she eliminated the mystery and detail of her Stanley Park forest interiors. Carr began to throw herself entirely into the process of painting. She interpreted the landscape through her own feelings about nature; she did not contrive the landscape to fit preconceived ideas and techniques. As she discarded her concern for convention and technique, a rhythmic spontaneity arose in her painting. She had resumed the progress begun in France by painting according to feeling, by attempting to show that there was something beneath the surface of the canvas. She had at last overcome the convention of the picturesque.

Emily Carr,
Wood Interior, 1909,
watercolour, 28¾ x 21⅝.
The Vancouver Art Gallery.

Emily Carr,
Indian Village, Ucluelet, 1898,
pen and ink, 8¼ x 11¾.
Provincial Archives, Victoria,
B.C.
▼

Emily Carr, ▶
Old Time Coast Village, ca.
1928,
oil on canvas, 36 x 50½.
The Vancouver Art Gallery.

In 1927 when Eric Brown invited Carr to participate in the "Exhibition of Canadian West Coast Art," she was prepared to benefit from contact with the Group of Seven. Travelling east for the opening of the exhibition, she viewed their work and felt "a little as if beaten at my own game." They had, she believed, found a unique style for interpreting the northern Ontario wilderness. Stripping the landscape bare, they had revealed the spirit, the "something bigger than fact,"[12] that she had so unsuccessfully sought in British Columbia. She readily identified with their struggle for public acceptance, their love of the Canadian wilderness and their belief that they had found a unique interpretation of it. Revi-

Emily Carr,
Deciduous Forest, ca. 1926,
oil on board, 15⅜ x 18¾.
Private Collection.

talized, especially by the work of Lawren Harris, who was "rising into serene, uplifted planes" where she longed to be, she returned to Victoria, and, at the age of fifty-seven, embarked on the most productive period of her career.[13]

Praised in Ottawa for her pre-1913 totem and village paintings, it was to those subjects that she now returned. The following summer she made a last, arduous trip to Indian villages on the Nass and Skeena rivers and the Queen Charlotte Islands. Back in Victoria she had barely an opportunity to begin working up her summer sketches when Mark Tobey arrived from Seattle. The impoverished Tobey came to The House of All Sorts in September of 1928 hoping to pick up a class. His prime pupil turned out to be Carr herself: "He told me to pep my work up and get off the monotone, even exaggerate light and shade, to watch rhythmic relations and reversals of detail."[14] At that time Tobey was obsessed with light, planes and volume. Carr did not bend to his obsession easily. There were rows; old habits had to be broken. Finally Carr went to him and admitted defeat.

Absorbing Tobey's teaching just months after her contact with the Group of Seven, Emily Carr's conception of the forest's form began to crystallize. The sculptured, densely packed, weighty and voluminous trees in "Old Time Coast Village" indicate that Tobey as well as Harris had taught her a great deal about light, volume and form. The forest, however, remained a peripheral concern until Harris told her to "give up Indian motifs" and to "create forms for yourself, direct from nature." She went "no more ... to the far villages, but to the deep, quiet woods near home where I sat staring, staring, staring."[15] In the woods Carr was able to find a motif that she could make distinctively her own. Her totem and village pictures had long dissatisfied her: "I was but copying the Indian idiom instead of expressing my own findings."[16] Camping in the forested parks around Victoria, she discovered what she could never have found in totemic forms—the living embodiment of God. The multitude of planes and swirls in her work all expressed, she wrote, "some attribute of God—power, peace, strength, serenity, joy."[17] She entered into the life of the trees, merging with nature, serving only as the instrument through which her God expressed itself.

Carr was attracted to the deep, wild and solitary places in the forest partly because few went there. Most people were, as she had been earlier, repelled by the forest's loneliness and density, frightened by its unsafe footing. She now felt that the trees were "better than we humans . . . more obedient to God," and took them as her closest friends.[18] For one who scoffed at relatives, was critical of friends and reproachful of artists, the forest was a private sanctuary. Immersing herself in the forest's midst, she harmonized the heavy undulating forest rhythms, capturing the spirit that had earlier mystified her.

While the forest was a sanctuary, Carr sometimes feared it. In her van amid the towering cedars at Goldstream Flats a short distance from Victoria, she wrote: "The cold clammy dark of this place is on me. . . . I suppose I'm a coward. I am not afraid exactly but it's creepy."[19] No painting expresses this ominous sentiment more than "Grey." Power, fear, an almost demonic or monstrous mood pervades the canvas. The source of light coming from within the tree, the cool colours and deep tones accompanying ascending lines create a hauntingly dramatic effect.

Although "Grey" echoes the static poster-presentation style of the late-twenties paintings of Harris and Tobey, Carr was not to be long under their spell. In 1932 she moved from the forest interior to the clearing where she found her own vocabulary. The surging underbrush brightened her palette, the wider sky introduced more light, the greater horizon and the broader field allowed for the play of the elements, and the syncopated rhythms of second-growth vegetation added yet another dimension. With colour transitions more gradual, forms subjected to the vibrations of light and air, her paintings such as "Forest Scene" sway, surge and sweep with a dynamism reminiscent only of her experimental paintings of the early 1920s. These forest-clearing works did not always express the freedom of growth. Many were didactic, preaching the great reverence she held for the wilderness, displaying her contempt for those who committed sacrilege against it. "Loggers Culls" is an explicit example of this, portraying a few skimpy trees that have been rejected by the forest's "executioners."[20]

In 1932 Carr asked herself: "Why don't I have a try at painting

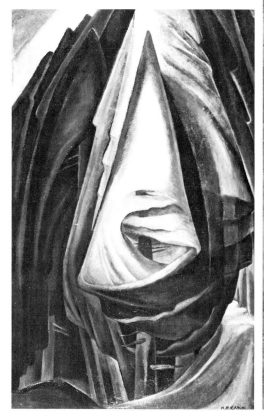

Emily Carr,
Forest Scene, ca. 1935,
oil on canvas, 32 x 27.
Collection of Mrs. Barbara C.
Kerr.

▲

Emily Carr,
Grey, ca. 1931,
oil on canvas, 43¾ x 27¼.
Collection of Mrs. Charles S.
Band.

rocks and cliffs and sea? Wouldn't it be good to rest the woods? Am I one-idea'd, small, narrow? God is in them all."[21] Carr's forest-clearing vocabulary was easily transferred to the Dallas Road cliffs near The House of All Sorts. In "Shoreline" everything pulsates. Yet a force beneath the surface of the painting connects sea to log, to cliff, to sky, to sea, making each a part of the whole and the whole a part of the breathing universe.

Amid the mountains that crushed upon Seton and Anderson lakes Carr was not so successful. "A feeling of stifle, of being trapped, of oppression and depression, of foreboding and awe" overcame her. She was unimpressed by A.Y. Jackson's mountains; she felt they were not right, yet was unable herself to express that "great dominating strength and spirit brooding there." She wrestled

with one mountain landscape from July to October in 1933. At times it would begin to move, to speak, then "suddenly it shifted, sulked, returned to obscurity, to smallness."[22] The beaches and the forests, not the mountains, were her elements.

Carr's blossoming came at a mature age. By the late 1930s when she had finally mastered her art of interpreting the West Coast forests and shores, recurring heart attacks and strokes gradually terminated her outdoor excursions. "I am beginning to get the tickle of Spring wanting to see the woods again," she wrote to a friend in 1941, but "don't know what I can do this year in sketching."[23] The immediacy of the forest was vital: the damp, rotting earth, the choking salal, the matronly cedars, the stillness, the silence. She liked her goods fresh, not canned, and too infrequent outings forced her return to the Indian theme. After the early 1940s she never painted in the woods again. More in than out of

Emily Carr,
Loggers Culls, 1935,
oil on canvas, 27 x 44.
The Vancouver Art Gallery.

Emily Carr,
Pemberton Meadows, no date,
oil on canvas, 35¾ x 26¾.
The Vancouver Art Gallery.

hospital, she devoted much time to writing, a talent which had accompanied her painting since her childhood.

For the greater part of her painting career Emily Carr perceived British Columbia through the English landscape tradition. Although French training helped to erode that perception, it did not offer anything more appropriate to the British Columbia landscape. She advanced largely through contact with the Fauve and Post-Impressionists in France and by her associations with the Pattersons, Tobey and the Group, but only her own intimate association with the landscape brought her development to the point where "things speak all over the place."[24]

Carr drew out of nature a more forceful and elementary order than British Columbians had previously recognized. She laid bare

"the underlying spirit, . . . the mood, the vastness, the wilderness" of the West.[25] In doing so she released herself and British Columbians from an imposed English vision which thought the wilderness to be gloomy and inhospitable. Jock Macdonald, who was also seeking a spiritual essence in the province's landscape, recognized Carr as "the first real genius from B.C." "I feel in her work," he wrote, "the first conscious expression of the rythum [sic] of life, relating this rythum [sic] to all nature, and definitely causing the observer . . . to be conscious of the fact that he or she is also related."[26]

Emily Carr,
Shoreline, ca. 1935,
oil on canvas, 27 x 44.
The McMichael Canadian
Collection, Kleinburg,
Ontario.

Chapter 8   Search for Form and Essence:
Vancouver 1925-45

While Emily Carr was the single most significant artist to force a new view of British Columbia's landscape upon its residents, she was not alone. In Vancouver there were several painters who were working toward similar ideas.

At the Vancouver School of Art, Charles Scott and Grace Melvin were adapting their painting to new ideas of landscape. Both were influenced by the Group of Seven and caught the Garibaldi Park fascination of F.H. Varley and Jock Macdonald, portraying the glaciers, peaks and lakes with clear colours and simple designs. Melvin, a designer in cloth and leather and an inimitable illuminator on vellum, consciously sought her patterns from nature. Nature, she felt, was a generous mother who offered boundless nourishment to the designer looking for form and colour. The designer must "feel himself as part of Nature—must merge himself

Charles H. Scott,
Floating Land, Garibaldi Park,
1927,
oil on panel, 11-15/16 x 15.
Private Collection.

in her unity." In the summer of 1927, while hiking in Garibaldi, she painted a picture which expressed the artist's need to "breathe Nature's rhythm and harmony."[1] With its flat design and vivid surface, its sharp lines and sweeping curves, "Red Mountain" recreated the simple pattern of the scene before her.

Scott, as principal of the Vancouver School of Applied and Decorative Art that had been founded in 1925, was burdened with teaching and school administration. Although he was allowed little time to paint, that which he did is a vivid testimony to his ability as well as to the modes of landscape perception and depiction which were changing between the two world wars. The broader style and brighter palette presaged in his 1927 "Floating Land, Garibaldi Park" took him further along the road toward penetrating the superficial appearance of the landscape. Flatter and more formal, "Gold and Blue Greys, Hornby Island" reflects his search for a lyrical mood, as much in atmosphere as in line and form.

Scott's eye often sought the vagaries of weather, catching, as in his Gulf Island watercolours, the moods and mutability of summer on the coast. Swirling, swooping clouds drifting toward sun-blistered sands mirror "all the tantalizing moods of Savary."[2]

During his decade in Vancouver, F.H. Varley was, without question, the most volatile, the most commanding influence on the local art scene. Tempestuous in temperament and art, he brought to Vancouver a formidable talent. Superb as a portraitist, he had been attracted to the possibilities of landscape by his Group colleagues. In British Columbia he continued his interest in the figure, but abandoned whatever tepidness he may have had about the Canadian landscape genre.

Varley, like W.J. Phillips, was raised amid the beauties of the Yorkshire landscape, among the beautiful crags, hills and moors, the dales and streams,[3] which roused his imagination. Restless and poetic, the young Varley studied art in Sheffield, then at the Antwerp Academy. Arthur Lismer, a Sheffield friend, told him of Toronto, and Varley, borrowing money, followed Lismer there in 1912. They worked together in the commercial art firm, Grip Limited, which also employed Tom Thomson, J.E.H. MacDonald, Frank Johnston and Frank Carmichael. In 1920 Varley was one of the little band of adventurers who formed the Group of Seven. He was revitalized by the North country; it came as a revelation to him.[4] But others of the Group felt that he "had no real love for the Canadian scene"; that he was unattracted to "the wild and the untamed to which the Group had hitched their wagon."[5]

It was portrait commissions in Winnipeg and Edmonton that took Varley west for the first time in 1924. He spent a few weeks in Calgary where, viewing the Rocky Mountains from high ground, he was impressed by their beauty. A trip to Banff extended his first flirtation with the western landscape and two years later he accepted Scott's offer to teach at the Vancouver School. He was excited at the longed-for opportunity "to live by the sea, have mountains at my back door and be sufficiently free from financial worries to experiment in paint."[6] "Ever since I saw the mountains at Banff," he told the *Province*, "I have wanted to come west."[7]

In British Columbia there was never any diffidence in Varley's attachment to landscape. From the day he arrived he was euphoric about "the immense possibility of the surrounding country." Vancouver, with its landscape setting, with its diversity of the oriental and occidental, could become the greatest art centre of Canada. "The whole country," he proclaimed, "is crying out to be painted."[8]

Intensely passionate toward all that he loved, Varley plunged into a fiery affair with the British Columbia landscape. He became an inveterate outdoorsman, painting in the woods or mountains virtually every weekend. He seldom allowed the climate to dampen his enthusiasm; rain, he said, only made the colours truer.[9] In his first summer he discovered Garibaldi Park. With Jock Macdonald and others he packed into the mountain peaks, first taking the boat to Squamish, the railway to Daisy Lake, then hiking straight in and up to the Black Tusk. Years later, Macdonald recalled his and Varley's discovery of the "unbelievably beautiful virgin country" of Garibaldi, "where six-thousand-foot meadows are carpeted with wild flowers, the lakes are pure emerald, the glaciers are fractured with rose-madder, turquoise-blue and indigo crevasses, and the mountains are black, ochre and Egyptian red." Carrying his sketching box, pup tent, sleeping bag and light rations, Varley hiked the fifteen miles from railhead. Overwhelmed by the immensity of nature, his city concerns faded: "The more he camped, the more he became part of the earth, of day and night and the diversified weather."[10]

Few have felt with more emotional intensity the vastness of the British Columbia landscape; few could have expressed it with as powerful a sentiment as Varley. "British Columbia is heaven," he wrote. "It trembles within me and pains with its wonder as when a child I first awakened to the song of the earth at home. Only the hills are bigger, the torrents bigger. The sea is here, and the sky is vast." Humans—"little bits of mind"—"clamber up rocky slopes, creep in and out of mountain passes," build little huts in sheltered places, "curl up in sleeping bags and sleep under the stars."[11] Varley conveyed this tremulous wonder to canvas in slashing strokes and impasto colour. His oils were always dry and textured, suggestive of the unpolished surfaces of rough-hewn

Grace Melvin,
Red Mountain and Garibaldi Lake, 1927,
guache on grey paper, 15 x 15. Collection of Miss Grace Melvin.

Charles H. Scott,
Gold and Blue Greys, Hornby Island, no date,
oil on canvas, 26⅜ x 31½. Art Gallery of Greater Victoria.

F.H. Varley,
Cheakamus Canyon, B.C., no date,
oil on panel, 11⅝ x 14¾. Collection of Mrs. Ross A. Lort.

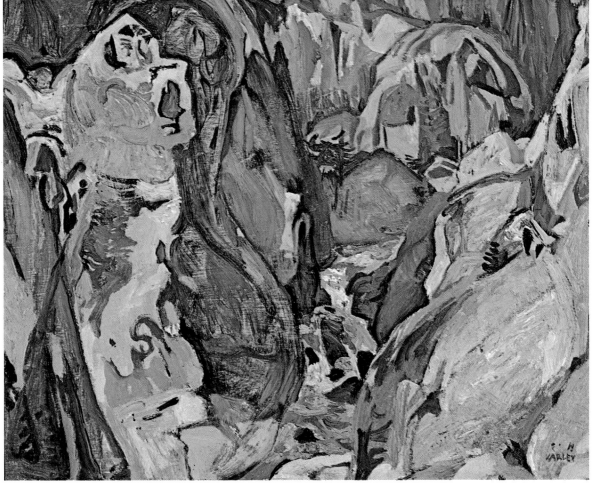

landscape. Intent upon form, he painted broadly, uncompromisingly suppressing detail to catch the inner power of the forms before him. With "moving form, majestically conceived,"[12] Varley sought to express the internal, the hidden meaning of the earth and sky. Art was not merely the recording of surface life. "The Artist divines the causes beneath";[13] he must "learn the laws of creation." Completely immersed in his surroundings, Varley had the power to grasp the most profound aspects of nature and express them in simple, basic terms.

Strong and vital as were his texture and his form, it was Varley's colour that was most distinctive. Varley had a personal theory of colour and he used a very special luminous emerald green to express the spirituality of nature. The ethereal, translucent greens of his Vancouver work are Varley's own, as individual as his thumb-print.

In Vancouver Varley found both the high and the low points of his life. It was here that he embraced fully the lure of landscape, here too that he met Vera, "the greatest single influence in my life."[14] But in 1933 he and Macdonald broke from the Vancouver School to found with Harry Täuber their own British Columbia College of Art. The stimulating free atmosphere, the wide-open premises, the success of attracting more students than the Vancouver School, were falsely promising. Hopelessly underfinanced in a depressed economy and fatally mismanaged by Varley and Täuber, the College failed after its second year. At about the same time as he was suddenly without an income, Varley parted from his wife. By December of 1935 he wrote from his Lynn Valley house of his longing "to get away from the dead & too trying conditions."[15] Scarcely able to afford tubes of paint, he hoped that a large canvas would bring him success in London "& release me, if possible, from this imprisoned life on the coast."[16] The artistic loneliness that he had felt since coming to Vancouver now overwhelmed him, yet his enthusiasm for the landscape did not diminish. "It's now 2 a.m. and warm as a summer night," he wrote on Boxing Day, 1935. "Snow on the peaks, soft rain in the valleys, mists playing tricks with the landscape & from the gorge below comes the sound of the Lynn in full flood." "Forgive the overflow," he added, it "must be the result of the full flood."[17]

F.H. Varley,
The Lions, ca. 1931,
oil on panel, 12 x 15.
The McMichael Canadian
Collection, Kleinburg,
Ontario.

Varley absorbed the heady winds of mountain, sea and sky and he passed on his yearning for elemental nature to his associates. In his students he aroused an intense creative fever, conveying to them an enthusiasm for the discovery and interpretation of form. Yet the Varley spell was not always wholesome; he preferred that students saw his way of doing things.[18] Few of his students ever freed themselves from Varley.

Although he tended to turn out imitators rather than creators, in Jock Macdonald Varley helped awaken a hidden artistic genius that found inspiration in Varley's love of the landscape. When Macdonald arrived in Vancouver in the summer of 1926, he came as a designer, not a painter. Born in 1897 at Thurso in the Scottish Highlands, he had received training in commercial design at the Edinburgh College of Art. Returning from war service at the front, he worked for a fabric and rug company in England, then took a position on the design staff of the Lincoln School of Art. In 1926 he accepted Scott's offer to come to the new Vancouver School.

Close contact with the small staff at the School, all of whom painted, encouraged Macdonald to try the medium. But it was Varley's enthusiasm for the landscape, for seeing it, being in it and painting it, that influenced him most directly. Macdonald came from a family of nature enthusiasts and his design, like Melvin's, was consciously tied to natural form. "Nature is after all the only and ever open book in matters of Design," he wrote in his first year in Vancouver. "She has more decorative forms than she can ever dispose of and we who would design must be ardent students of her." He was enthusiastic about the potential of British Columbia's landscape. "Glory in the beauty of your country," he told Vancouver students, "for all the big forces of Nature are around you." Although the inspiration from nature, the feeling for form, the ability to "extract all there is to know about any one of God's creatures"[19] was already in Macdonald, the grasping of painting technique and the suppression of acquired design habits were a struggle. He had difficulty achieving the same colour values in oil that he could attain with facility in poster paint, and regretted that design forms, colour combinations and commercial mannerisms were "saturated in my blood." He accepted Varley's encouragement, but shied away from his persuasive dominance, from being led too far "along certain avenues." In the end, Macdonald preferred "to stand on my own legs & by so doing, sink or swim."[20]

Macdonald never completely eradicated his design mannerisms. In pictures like "Garibaldi Lake" the design influence emerges as formalist, flat and petrified. The rigidity of the mode restricted Macdonald's search for spiritual meaning in paint. Yet it was the paint medium that he hoped to master; it offered the visual luminosity and purity of colour that could give to art "a sort of spiritual uplifting quality." By 1935 his greatest ambition was to obtain on canvas that kind of spiritual experience.[21]

Repelled by Vancouver's dreary, materialistic urban life, Macdonald sought escape, after the failure of the British Columbia college, at Nootka on the remote west coast of Vancouver Island. But eventually the cash imperative, as well as weakened health, drove him back to Vancouver's "drab and meaningless existence" where spiritual expression had been "smothered by the masses."[22]

Anxious not to fall victim to the smothering stagnation of city life, Macdonald became increasingly concerned with spiritual values during his time in British Columbia. He studied eastern philosophies and read the works of Schopenhauer and Ospensky. Although Macdonald felt that there existed a fourth dimension beyond conventional reality, he was convinced that the extra dimension and inner reality could only be apprehended by a close attention to external appearance. Appearances remained "the key to a deep and mysterious reality."[23]

The landscape was a necessity and a stimulation. "In my new art experiments," he wrote, "I have to live with Nature, be in constant touch with its life forces."[24] Although denied a meaningful teaching role in Vancouver and thus forced to search for work anywhere, after a trip to California he was even more convinced that "British Columbia is the land of inspiration."[25] Back in Garibaldi in 1938, he found its attraction undiminished by six visits. There was nothing like Garibaldi, "with its meadows, flowers,

J.W.G. Macdonald,
Garibaldi Lake, B.C., 1932,
pen and ink, 6¾ x 9.
Private Collection.

peacock coloured meadow pools and lakes, emerald green glacier lakes, four glaciers, black volcanic necks of rock; red cinder, pale ochre shale, and blue mountains." He had discovered Sphinx Glacier and was in "amazing wonder of it" for days. Sphinx was "the most powerful force that I have ever seen outside the mountainous waters of the open Pacific." It was "simply marvellous" in its tortured forms, block massed ice, iridescent caves, open crevasses, pressure thrusts, and constantly thundering crashes of ice walls.[26]

Macdonald's exhilaration over the British Columbia landscape was tempered by financial difficulties. In 1946 after years of living a minimal existence, even suffering malnutrition, he taught in Calgary and then settled in Toronto. Neither the hardships in British Columbia nor his departure diminished his affection for the province and the landscape that had initially inspired him. On going to Toronto he vowed that he would never become an eastern artist—"my love is too deeply rooted in B.C."[27]

Other artists of the generation of Macdonald and Varley, though less intensely involved in the spiritual philosophies of the age, also sought to capture the landscape in forms and colours that were abstracted from superficial appearance. In style and feeling, Paul Rand's work most closely approximated the landscape painting of Macdonald.

Rand was born in Bonn, Germany, in 1896 and was sent to Canada by his father for a two-year trip in 1912. Caught by the outbreak of war as an enemy alien, Rand remained in Canada, cut off from his family who misunderstood his "unpatriotic" failure to answer the German call to arms.

After working as a builder in Coleman, Alberta, Rand moved to Vancouver in 1926. Taking evening study at the Vancouver School under Macdonald, Varley and W. P. Weston, he found work as a commercial artist, first on an irregular free-lance basis, then as art director of the *Sun* and ultimately with Evergreen Press.

Like Macdonald's landscapes, Rand's work had close affinities with the mainstream of Canadian and American art of the twenties and thirties. The canvases of Thomas Hart Benton and others of the American Scene movement show similar stylistic elements and share the same feeling for regional identities. Rand's feeling for the region's landscape was evidenced in a watercolour of "Crow's Nest Mountain," done a few years after moving to Vancouver. The border mountain stands in solitary amplitude, snow covering only its sloping areas while twisting cliffs push up vertically toward a brooding sky. The picture is a study in mass—the sky is as voluminous as the mountain and its surrounding hills. The brush technique is unusual, its dappling verticals emphasize the upward thrust of earth mass and counter the strong horizontal lines of the grey-clouded sky.

Rand's later work, while retaining its strong and dramatic form, stressed the more lyrical elements of the landscape. In quiet seas, silent driftwood, the rhythms of lakes and hills, the pleasing colour of autumn maples, the rich splendour of a forest interior, Rand found subjects for his love of the local surroundings. In "Sombre Skies, Anvil Island" he found a perfect expression for his mood. George Vancouver had found Howe Sound sublime but gloomy; Rand invested the grey-clouded scene with a sombre serenity. In this painting and others he demonstrated a mastery of sky effects, chiselling his clouds into round volumes or sending them swirling and dancing across the sky. At times they radiate light, circling up to the centre of the canvas.

Rand and Macdonald both travelled to the Okanagan where they received inspiration from the area's bold contours and shimmering atmosphere. While Rand emphasized its colourfulness, finding in the hills a character that the valleys, too cultivated and new, lacked, Macdonald found a strong Van Gogh quality in the sun-baked hills and dry sagebrush. Macdonald's Okanagan canvases emphasize lakes and hills set against big skies filled with cloud variations.

Many of the painters who reached their artistic maturity in the years following 1926 drew the substance of their work out of the landscape's forms, endowing it with a solidity, a surging rhythm, often a heroic mould. In this search for essential structure and meaning, W.P. Weston's paintings could be identified by their simple dramatization of the vital forces of nature—of trees defiant against the elements, of mountains standing boldly against the ho-

Paul Rand,
Crow's Nest, 1932,
watercolour, 12⅛ x 15-3/16
(sight).
Private Collection.

Paul Rand,
Sombre Skies, Anvil Island, 1933,
oil on board, 18½ x 24½.
Private Collection.

J.W.G. Macdonald,
*Thunder Clouds over Okanagan
Lake, B.C.,* 1944-5,
oil on canvas, 28 x 34.
The National Gallery of
Canada, Ottawa.

W.P. Weston,
Defiance, 1949,
oil on board, 34 x 38.
Collection of Mrs. Doris
Wood.

rizon, of driftwood thrown up by the sea.

Weston arrived in Vancouver from London in 1909 to teach at King Edward High School. From there he moved on to the city's Provincial Normal School where he remained until his retirement in 1946. Initially he painted in the "English manner" of his London training, but within a few years he became dissatisfied with his work. "I wanted to paint Canada," he said years later, "and I realized I wasn't doing it."[28] By 1929 Weston had radically altered his style from sterile academicism to a linear, spatial and decorative style consonant with the regional North American manner. Weston had, wrote one reviewer, "out-grouped the Group."[29]

Weston was concerned with form and structure and inspired by the wild and the defiant. Even more than Rand and Macdonald, he defined his volumes, emphasized mass, found an internal structure, felt the swell and rhythm of his surfaces. He was able to determine how a sense of structure operated within the roots, mountains and trees that he portrayed. He moulded and sculpted his forms, revealing their essential tactile quality. His mountains were not, as Fripp's had been, clothed in mists and vapours. They stood unobscured and immovable.

Within the wildness of nature, it was the monumentality of a mountain and the struggling life-force of a tree that most enticed Weston. Frequently tree and mountain were combined—a powerful, solitary tree stretching, in the convention of the period, vertically through the centre of the canvas. "Wild-armed pines and stoic slabs of rock"[30] became his subjects. "I like trees that have had a struggle," he said, "the trees along the seashore or up on the mountains."[31] They had character, almost an anthropomorphic character. They were like people who had had to fight to live, whose struggle was visible in the tortured twists and shapes of their torsos. Some may have perished in the struggle, dead now, but still standing defiant against the elements. One saw in the dead tree the internal dynamics of struggle—"all the muscles and growth of that tree disclosed."[32] In the mountains of British Columbia, even more than in its trees, Weston found the archetypal patterns of primitive nature that he sought. They too possessed an underlying anatomical form—swelling muscles, bulging shoulders, a skeletal structure of spinal rock.

Weston's view of British Columbia was heroic. Even his titles—"Life Force," "Battle Scarred," "Unvanquished"—are epic. This was the way he came to view the landscape around him, as vast, untamed, virtually untouched by man. He had been brought up on "the old civilized landscape," but in British Columbia he found something different: "Nature as it could be—in the raw—before man interfered with it."[33] There are no humans in Weston's pictures and only rarely boats or houses as evidences of man. Civilization, the human figure, was irrelevant to his primitivist conception of the new-world landscape around him. Like Varley's "little bits of mind" against the huge environment, Weston felt that the mountains and forests "are so gigantic that man seems puny & his slight inroads are comparatively insignificant."[34] He was unattracted to the Fraser Valley—it reminded him of the old country with its orderly farms and fields; he wanted to get into the mountains where things "hadn't been touched."[35] An artist in British Columbia, responding as he must to his surroundings, "cannot but record the overwhelming preponderance of nature & omit the human element."[36]

As Carr captured the British Columbia forest interior, Weston caught the mountains. He also did forest interiors, some of luscious beauty, but his forte was his solitary trees and stupendous mountains. Some of Weston's qualities came from his method. An inveterate sketcher, he nevertheless depended upon his memory. The single most important lesson he had retained from his formal training was an ability to paint from memory. In England he had been taught to draw from a model, then after an hour, to draw the same subject from memory. Always, he said, the second sketch was better than the first. Only when he was in a new area, like Fernie and the Kootenay in the 1950s, did Weston go back to painting out-of-doors. "Otherwise," he said, "I paint from memory and sketches."[37] His well-trained memory singled out the salient aspects of a scene, its essential structure. For his mountain sketches, Weston often relied upon a telescope. Through its magnifying lens he caught, perhaps better than through the naked eye, the peaks and ridges of the disembodied giants.

Inspired by the same romantic notion of wilderness, imbued with a sense of stylized form that often became decorative and flat, Weston has sometimes been put down as being derivative of the Group of Seven. He was irked by the assumed similarity. He asserted that his mature style was the result of a personal struggle to overcome acquired habits, and an inbred perception of nature. He and other British Columbia artists, Weston insisted, were cut off from the parallel developments in central Canada: "We had to work it out for ourselves. We were doing it by the time we saw the Group of Seven."[38] In fact, Weston's landscapes are similar to those of his eastern contemporaries, especially Frank Carmichael and A.J. Casson, only by reason of time and place. He, too, reacted against English traditionalism and, selecting and adapting other influences, evolved an objective style that was "regional" or "national" in its inspiration but international in its appeal. Rand, Macdonald and Weston searched for "a compact, massive, and

W.P. Weston,
Mount Cheam, ca. 1940,
oil on canvas, 28 x 36.
Collection of Mrs. Barbara C.
Kerr.

rhythmical composition of forms" determined by line.[39] It was the same style practised by American Scene artists, by the Englishman Christopher Perkins in New Zealand, and was not unlike that of Stanley Spencer in Britain. To trace the influences would be complex and impossible. Regionalism attached itself to local life and local landscape as its subject matter, and, because it was unavoidable after Cézanne, to form—volume, space, mass and line. In this Weston was no more derivative than the Group itself.

This generation of landscape painters in British Columbia— Scott, Varley, Macdonald, Rand, Weston and, of course, Emily Carr, revolutionized the perception of landscape. All had a keen ability to perceive nature through the search for structure; all sharpened the faculties of observation. All sought, as one of the fundamental purposes of art, "to heighten man's instinctive awareness of the cosmos and to enable him to identify himself with the vast range of things within the universe."[40] Their universe began within the province, but it did not end there. They sought its peculiar order and essence, but they also went beyond the interpretation of a province to the universality of nature and of nature's man. After Weston's archetypal mountains and twisted trees, after Carr's rhythmic forests and sweeping beaches, no artist and few laymen could see these facets of nature in quite the same way. The artist, as Weston put it, "should reveal to people what they had not noticed,"[41] what they had not seen. The perception of nature had begun to imitate art.

Chapter 9   An End — or a Beginning?

After Carr, after Weston, after Varley, after Rand and Macdonald, landscape painting in British Columbia had an impetus and a continuity of its own. It continued to react to outside influences, to be affected by impulses from beyond its mountain barrier and its southern border, but it reflected an indigenous landscape tradition. The generation of artists and teachers who reached their artistic maturity in the late twenties and early thirties had discovered the landscape anew, and, feeling that they had penetrated to its essence, they found a new interpretation of its forests, coasts and mountains in rhythmic contours and stylized forms. That generation had come to terms, conceptually and artistically, with the landscape of British Columbia.

The younger generation of the mid 1900s, growing up under the tutelage and influence of the Group of Seven, Macdonald,

Weston and especially Varley and Carr, adopted this new conception and vision. As Vito Cianci, a student at the Vancouver School, wrote in 1928, the artist of "the real British Columbia" had found its true character, not in placid pools or sunny garden spots, "but in the boundless sweep of sky and country away from man's depressing influence." Cianci prescribed subjects that were wild and elemental—exactly those which the younger artists sought in emulation of their masters:

> The majestic curve of shore and wave upon a calm beach; the lines of mountain and mist across the water; the relentless upward thrust of rounded hills; trees gnarled and twisted and blighted by the breath of forest fire, silhouetted against dull skies; wave forms magically created in swirls of snow; gaunt stumps; dead branches grotesquely mingling with brilliant new growth of fireweed; all that Nature has to offer in such profusion calls to him and he responds joyously.

The mystique of basic form and line could only be captured by the artist who had eyes "open to the true character of the country," who "feels and understands its rhythm, and his spirit is one with that of his surroundings." No sitting with lunch basket, watercolour box and parasol in Stanley Park. The real artist sought intimacy with his mountain, climbing it, searching it, exploring it, making "every contour and hollow and crevice his own, and part of him."[1]

Growing up within Victoria's gentility, but bristling with cultural ideas, Jack Shadbolt, Max Maynard, Roy Daniells and others formed a singular group of young people interested in the creative arts. Shadbolt recalled how "several of us kindred spirits" drifted together because of a mutual interest in contemporary art of all kinds. Gathering around Victoria High School principal Ira Dilworth for literary soirées and later forming their own group called the Fossils, they read and discussed the English Romantics, "the usual route of Shelley, Wordsworth or Keats." They took long walks in the country, sketching and making notes. They spent late evenings listening to music, reading poetry; evenings which were "enormously powerful in the formation period of one's own psyche." Those evenings were "rhapsodic"; it was "a marvelous time."[2]

Max Maynard,
Pines and Rocks, 1943,
oil on paper, 18½ x 23.
Private Collection.

Already romantic about the landscape, they fell in with Emily Carr. Max Maynard was the first to walk into Carr's solo show in the basement of the Crystal Gardens in 1930. He had seen isolated paintings previously but never full walls of her sweeping forests. The effect was tremendous. A young school teacher alive to modern trends yet short of exposure, he found in Carr an exemplar. She and Maynard became friends, and he took Shadbolt to Carr's Simcoe Street studio, where they became frequent visitors: "She never said a great deal, but let us chatter away."[3] Carr was too possessive of "her" landscape and too uninterested in studio talk to warm to the young men. She resented "Maxi & Jackie,"[4] who held their province's landscape in similar reverence, yet sought to analyze, dissect and intellectually explore its attractions. But the difference of temperament did not prevent the youthful artists from admiring and emulating the great artist in their midst.

Maynard's sketches show both his affinity with and independence from Carr. His feeling for line and form brought coherence to the lifeless trees in an untitled 1942 pencil drawing. From the mid-forties, however, literary interests dominated his life; pursuing an academic career he moved to Winnipeg and then to New Hampshire.

To Jack Shadbolt, Maynard was "one of my mentors."[5] From Maynard, an artistic and literary man five years his senior, Shadbolt could and did learn a great deal. Maynard's introduction of Shadbolt to the burnt-over areas around the Sooke Hills—the twisted roots, the black soil, the fireweed—was the latter's first real awakening to the landscape.[6] Though both were struck by the strength of the early drawings of the English artist, Paul Nash, and influenced by the Group of Seven, their respect for Carr was even greater. Shadbolt's interest in tree forms "grew into something compelling under the image of her brooding, visceral and vaulted interior spaces of the rain forest."[7]

The exposure of Carr through her 1930 solo show, the presence of eager young artists like Shadbolt and Maynard and the more recent arrival of Lodewyk Bosch and Ina D.D. Uhthoff, added colour to the genteel Victoria milieu. Bosch arrived from Holland in 1930 to visit his Victoria aunt. Known as both an artist and critic he brought with him the mystique of the European *avant-garde*. A woman who had a greater impact on the community was Scottish-born Ina D.D. Uhthoff. Like Grace Melvin and Charles Scott, Uhthoff had attended the Glasgow School of Art when the influence of the Scottish designers Charles Rennie Mackintosh and Maurice Griffenhagen was at its height. Marriage to a Canadian volunteer at the close of the war brought her to the Kootenay Lake district where the landscape was "crying out to be recorded in pencil, paint, oils and watercolours."[8] Relocating in Victoria in 1926 she taught art in private schools before opening her own teaching studio. In 1928, her one-woman staff expanded to include a destitute Mark Tobey, then boarding with Emily Carr. Enrolling in his classes herself, Uhthoff "gained a new visoon [sic]," but "didn't have time to develop it as I was so busy."[9] Teaching, writing art columns for the *Colonist* and organizing with Mark Kearley The Little Centre, the progenitor of the Art Gallery of Greater Victoria, she nevertheless left a large cache of unsold paintings and drawings at her death in 1971. One conté sketch, "Cedar," shows an affinity with the styles of Carr, Maynard and Shadbolt. Unlike Maynard and Shadbolt, however, Uhthoff did not dissect and intellectually analyze the elements of nature, but sought expression of the surface reality of the landscape, capturing the lyricism of nature's patterns.

The division between the modern and traditional elements of Victoria was most clear in 1932 when Maynard, becoming the vice-president of the Arts and Crafts Society, arranged a "modern room" to be part of the annual exhibition. Carr, Shadbolt, Maynard, Uhthoff, Edythe Hembroff, a figurative painter, and Ronald Bladen, a student of Maynard's later to become an eminent New York sculptor, gathered together to form the first integrated exhibition of modern trends in Victoria. Its effect was, however, minimal. Maynard's vice-presidency did not extend to the following year. Though Carr remained in Victoria until her death in 1945, Shadbolt and Maynard soon moved to Vancouver. Uhthoff, too entrenched in teaching, had little opportunity to develop that new vision of Mark Tobey. Victoria returned to its slumber.

The young artists of Vancouver, graduates mostly of the Vancouver School or the British Columbia College, were similarly romantic and earnest. Varley was the great inspiration, the "Master," the teacher who "made you feel that, God! This is the most wonderful thing to be doing!"[10] For the most part the younger generation reacted against the drabness of the city, against its "artificiality," its toil, its worry, and sought a spirituality in elemental nature. The essays, verse and stories of *The Paint Box*, the annual of the Vancouver School, expressed this élan as students wrote of their kinship to mountain souls, of sitting in solitude and looking down from a mountain upon the heartaches and failures of the city. Near the sky, above the toil and strife, the smoke, dust and noise were left behind. Up near the peaks of silent mountains, dark with great pines, by lakes and along lost trails and moss-covered rocks—"To these great joys/I give my heart."[11] The young poet Earle Birney felt the same fascination in "David," for whom mountains "were made to see over." On his Waterton Lakes holi-

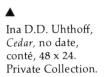

Ina D.D. Uhthoff,
Cedar, no date,
conté, 48 x 24.
Private Collection.

Irene Hoffar Reid,
*Store–Mt. Gardner, Bowen
Island,* 1935,
11-3/16 x 11⅝.
Collection of Mrs. Irene
Hoffar Reid.

◀ Edward Hughes,
Climbing, 1930,
lino cut, 8½ x 7½.
Vancouver School of Art, *The
Paint Box*, Vol. V (1930), p. 8.

▲

Jack Shadbolt,
Tree and Hills, 1940,
conté, 18⅞ x 24.
Private Collection.

day, Birney escaped

> . . . from the straight
> shrieking roads, the square fields,
> the cubed implacable factory and the unendable hurry.[12]

Such have been the dreams of many young people since Wordsworth, but never more so than among this generation of nature-worshipping students fed on a Group-like mystique and initiated into it by their Vancouver masters. One could feel, wrote Cianci about camping at the Black Tusk with Varley, "an indefinable sense of being not merely a spectator in this, Nature's magnificent display, but an essential part of it all; a feeling of absolute unity with all the gorgeous manifestations of the surroundings."[13]

E. J. Hughes, a student at the Vancouver School, contributed a lino-cut of a mountain climber to the 1930 *Paint Box*. A powerful picture, the figure becomes part of the landscape, making "every contour and hollow and crevice his own, and part of him." Irene Hoffar, trained under the discriminating eye of Varley, but also an admirer of Scott, painted figures as well as landscape. Her favourite sketching grounds were more often the shacks under Burrard Bridge than the mountain vastness, but she found some of her best terrain in the unspoiled beauty of Bowen Island. Very much under Varley's influence, her sketches caught the strength of the rocks and trees. Shadbolt, in Vancouver teaching at Kitsilano Junior High, also fell under Varley's influence. He remembers Varley as a passionate and poetic man—"talking to him reinforced all my romantic tendencies to an overall rhythm and toward evocatively sensuous colour and pigmentation." The dominant tree trunk and closely packed hill profile of a 1940 Vancouver sketch by Shadbolt are aspects "traceable to Varley," but "combined with influences from Carr."[14]

Other aspects of the province were investigated by eager students and artists. Fred Amess painted the Gulf Island strand, Margaret Williams the rocky coast of Howe Sound, Margaret Lougheed the hills of the Cariboo. Jim Dickie drew rhythmically poised bare trees, while Alistair Bell's ink or drypoint studies of sea islands and tidal waters and B.C. Binning's shoreline scenes were also becoming familiar.

This ecstatic exploration of British Columbia's nature was cut short. Lithe balsam fingers became as "gaunt as a Jew's in Poland" and the sun setting over the Gulf of Georgia rushed down through Asian skies, "garish/ with burst of shell and unarrested rocket," burning Libyan sands "red with libations poured to the guns."[15] Almost all the younger generation went into uniform. Shadbolt, Hughes, Paul Goranson, Peter Aspell, Orville Fisher and Molly Lamb became war artists, far away from their province. Goranson's ship was torpedoed from under him in the Atlantic, Fisher landed at Normandy on D-Day, and August Roozeboom, a Dutch-born student of the Vancouver School of Art, died while serving with Dutch airborne commandoes. The older artists were also affected. While reasserting a dedication to the expression of "beauty and truth" as "the most essential qualities of life,"[16] they worked on the home front. "I am district warden of Capilano," reported Macdonald, "Lawren [Harris] is Special Cop, Amess a Commando Ranger, Scott in A. R. P. & so on."[17] Emily Carr sewed ladies' pajamas for refugees in England and "Bommed drawers" for "pretty well every woman in London, Coventry & Liverpool."[18] Weston, Macdonald and Harris contributed silk-screen landscape posters for the walls of army messes, and Scott dedicated the summer of 1942 to recording army life at Nanaimo and Gordon Head.

For those abroad the British Columbia landscape had never seemed so peaceful. Birney, sitting under English skies, could recall a heaven

> where nothing whirled more savagely
> than kittiwakes by Nootka seas
> ...where no sound stabbed
> the innocent ear more stridently
> than killdeer's or the chickadee's.[19]

*   *   *   *

By the close of the war, British Columbia art had reached a mature stage, a "coming of age" which denoted both a "wider general knowledge of aesthetic principles and a pronounced blossoming of creative local talent."[20] In 1945 Emily Carr, by then solidly recognized as British Columbia's most significant artist, died in her seventy-fourth year. Weston and Macdonald were established in "their respective, crystallized scenic styles"[21] and the latter left for Calgary in 1946. At the 1943 Vancouver exhibitions there were "new notes of mature achievements" and a conviction that "no part of Canada is more alive artistically today than this western province."[22] British Columbia was sufficiently advanced by 1944 to have rebel artists organize their own *salon des refusés* of pictures rejected by the Vancouver Art Gallery's jury.

Their outlook altered by new experience, British Columbia's war artists returned to resume their interrupted careers. Shadbolt, back from bombed London and the shock of concentration camp photographs, relieved his revulsion in macabre images. E.J. Hughes, back from war service in England and Kiska, found a home on Vancouver Island and there carried on in the interwar realist tradition. Young veterans of the war, like Bruno Bobak and Gordon Smith, settled on the coast. Smith, married to a Vancouver girl, moved to the city in 1944 after recuperating from war injuries received in Sicily. Bobak, married to Molly Lamb, found a position at the Vancouver School of Art.

The artistic continuity had not been lost, but after the war, the vigour and élan of new discovery was spent. By the end of the 1940s the landscape became a passive inspiration to motorists or was vulgarized when "Beautiful British Columbia" became a licence-plate catch-phrase and later was put between full-colour covers of a government glossy. A firm tradition remained, but it had lost much of its freshness and vitality. Forest suburb living in indoor-outdoor houses reconciled the urban with nature while the city itself lost that revulsion which had driven the previous generation into the woods and mountains. Vancouver, with its jazz clubs and theatres, developed into an alive and enticing city. Some saw it as a place of the "lonely crowd," so captured by Donald Jarvis' pictures of empty men in crowded streets. This was, however, as much a transferred New York as a British Columbia image. More lyrically, John Korner's "Favourite Harbour" series reconciled city and landscape by presenting a jewel-like Vancouver, floating in a radiant setting of water, mountains and sky. Shadbolt, who, like

B.C. Binning,
Old Maple Tree, 1944,
pen and ink, 18 x 24.
The National Gallery of
Canada, Ottawa.

E.J. Hughes,
Finlayson Arms, 1965,
oil on canvas, 32 x 48.
Dominion Gallery, Montreal.

several others, built studio-houses on the forest fringe of the city, immersed himself in the nature of his immediate surroundings. Digging into the earth for a foundation and septic tank, he became excited at viewing layers of soil at eye-level. The minute forms of life—worms and insects, seeds and pods—inspired a series of nature-cycle paintings. The most imperceptible embryonic features of nature were transposed into something "symbolic of the large world and large meanings."[23]

John Korner,
Coast Nocturne, no date,
oil on canvas, 46¼ x 34.
The Vancouver Art Gallery.

Jack Shadbolt,
Remnants of a Dry Season, 1949,
watercolour, 37 x 26¾.
The Vancouver Art Gallery.

The trends of the fifties extended into the next decade. The sprawl of suburbs to the south and east of Vancouver and to the north and west of Victoria, the suburbanization of interior cities like Prince George, Kamloops and the Okanagan towns, were attestations to the decline of landscape values. The cities and towns preserved little of their scenery save a clamouring desire for a view—as often of extensive "manscape" as of natural landscape. Despite the provincial government's talk of wilderness land and natural conservation areas, it bargained away provincial parks to mining companies, reducing parkland by two million acres. Increased leisure brought more weekend recreation while affluence created intense pressures upon the landscape in the form of automobiles, recreation vehicles, power boats and snowmobiles. The landscape content in art suffered even more. One curator judged that "landscape has disappeared and with it any claim to regionalism" in British Columbia painting.[24] Symptomatically, the younger artists of the sixties, practitioners of the newer trends from New York and California, tended "to find living and working quarters

Toni Onley,
Shadow Cove, Galiano Island,
1975,
watercolour, 11¼ x 15.
Collection of the artist.

Gordon Smith,
West Coast R 4, 1976,
acrylic on canvas, 60 x 72.
Collection of the artist.

right in the commercial areas of the city ... rather than the city's fringes."[25] Their art was gestural or formal, expressive of subjective emotion or problems of colour and form. Hard-edged or geometric, mystical madalas or swirling collages, the art of the sixties was far removed from external nature. As art became independent of any external image, it developed into a "negation of nature."[26] Where landscape images remained, they were made purposely empty or mischievously scornful.

The works of Gary Lee Nova and Iain Baxter were parodies of the landscape. Nova might use the symbols of landscape—flowers, rainbow, clouds—but he arranged them artificially on a geometric format. Baxter went further, using plastic to vacuum mould bas-relief mountains, sky and sea. In 1966 he put an inflated vinyl cloud, some water and toy plastic boats in a vinyl bag to create "Bagged Landscape with 4 Boats." The British Columbia landscape had become a plastic plaything. Baxter proposed a white vinyl cap cover to be put on a Rocky Mountain when its snow melted. "I feel," he wrote, that "I am the new Hudson River School traditionalist, using water, air, sky, land, clouds and boats."[27] The tendency to mock the land was carried even further. Nova created a mirror waterfall in 1969 by placing a trapezoid mirror in a stream to form a waterfall that would reflect sky and autumn leaves. An article about the experiment, subtitled "the artist as ecologist," recorded that "the artist predicted that children would smash the mirror with rocks. They did."[28]

Baxter poured paint and barium grease into the ground, created sculptures by peeling moss from fallen trees and prepared to float styrofoam labels down rivers and on lakes. Another "ecological project" was to black out, using a plastic tarp, one acre of forest until all vegetation wilted or died. Under Baxter's advice George Sawchuck also participated in this "reshaping and reperception of landscape and ecologies." Sawchuck went about putting bicycle wheels in trees and embedding various pieces of junk ("found objects") in tree bark. "I love woods—a tree is a living thing," Sawchuck said in a 1969 interview. He liked seeing "how the trees take these things and start to kind of cover them up, because you can always see where there has been a clothes-line tied to a tree, how it's choked the tree but yet it comes together again."[29]

The "ecological" word-play of these mockeries was drawn from the new environmental concern which began to appear in the late sixties. Environmentalism received new vigour through the formation of organizations to fight pollution and of a British Columbia branch of the powerful, California-based Sierra Club. The Greenpeace Foundation began its fight for the marine environment with a demonstration against the nuclear tests on Alaska's Amchitka Island. The environmental movement had some successes, but the vulnerability of the landscape was revealed in the need to legislate the preservation not only of wilderness, but even of agricultural land.

Some painters reflected the concerns of the late sixties by returning to the landscape. Among the first was Toni Onley. A brilliant abstract collagist earlier in the decade, Onley later began to introduce landscape images into his pictures. By 1970 his landscapes had become explicit and identifiable as beach logs, sand, trees and rocks. Landscape motifs reappeared in the works of other artists who had passed through periods of hard-edged abstractionism, notably B.C. Binning and Gordon Smith. Inspired by the "Ocean Park" seascapes of San Franciscan Richard Diebenkorn, Smith began to use images of British Columbia's shore and sea. He warned, however, that "people should not think that I am trying to record this landscape. To me it still is where I'm using paint and I'm using colour. It's an abstract thing."[30]

The landscape remained an abstraction, even among the artists who, in the seventies, were returning more and more to it. George Tiessen and Myron Jones presented landscape silhouettes; Richard Prince, Carol Thompson and Ken Wallace created hard-edged compositions that, while abstract, were definitely discernable as headlands, forests or hills and clouds. The terrain seemed sterile, denatured, distant and empty—a springboard for the artists' preoccupation with colour and form. Yet the landscape as subject matter had returned to many British Columbia artists just when a concern for the province's environment was acknowledged by many of its people. As more artists of diverse styles find a new visual experience in landscape, it seems that British Columbians are on the verge of another cycle of perception, perhaps a renewal of the ineffable bonds that tie people to the landscape about them.

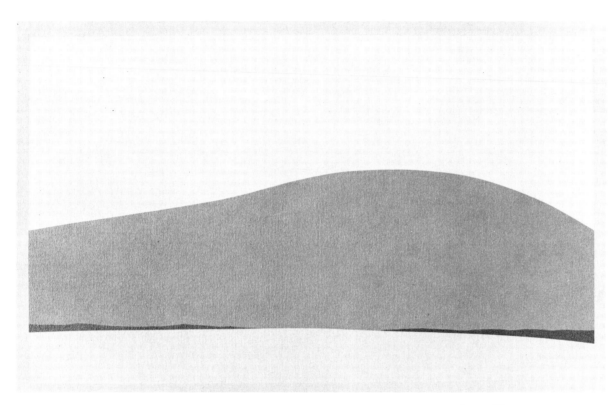

George Tiessen,
Saltspring, 1975,
acrylic on canvas, 16 x 26.
Collection of the artist.

Epilogue

The perception of the British Columbia landscape has changed radically since the day Cook sailed along the coast. To the early Europeans its dreary monotony and apparent inhospitality gave an appearance of repellent desolation. The first explorers were accustomed to seeking beauty and aesthetic satisfaction in parklands which bore the print of man, of European habitation, of cottages, mansions and villages. That stamp of human artifice was what attracted James Douglas and others to Victoria's "Eden" in the midst of an otherwise dreary wilderness. While the formidable nature of the landscape could give an impression of sublimity, the prevailing impression of the surroundings was bleak and forlorn. Eventually the great mountains began to dominate the human perception. Often vulgarized, they appealed to the romanticism of the nineteenth century as exotic elements of the wilderness which, with the gigantic forests, challenged the standards of those who continued to seek beauty in traditional terms. The wilderness itself began to have its own romantic associations.

In the twentieth century, wilderness became a virtue. It was extolled in sport, by mountaineers, in scout and woodcraft movements. The wilderness became the cure for the crowded city. In Canada it was the age of Grey Owl, Earnest Thompson Seton, Vilhjalmur Stefansson and Tom Thomson, men who met the challenge of wilderness solitude. The Group of Seven adapted this romantic worship of the savage land to their art. The artistic vision strayed from cultivation and artifice to an appreciation of the solitude and solemnity of the rugged and the wild. Even parklands became not the gentle undulating lawns dotted with groves of trees, but wilderness parks like Algonquin and Yoho. Large portions of Vancouver's Stanley Park were kept as a "permanent preserve of wilderness and the virtues of *le sauvage heureux et bon*," far distant in conception from Regents Park or the Bois de Boulogne.[1] The wilderness developed its own mystique, its own spirituality. Mixing Wordsworth with Thoreau, Whitman and theosophy, a mystical, even occult, view of nature and the landscape was expressed by artists such as Carr, Varley and Macdonald.

The eighteenth and nineteenth centuries had desired evidence of man's presence in the landscape. The early twentieth century almost denied man's right to be there. British Columbia artists found their material "in rugged nature, instead of man's developments." Weston felt that the province's trees and mountains "so outscale man & his works that one hardly notices his presence," and Shadbolt noted that "perhaps it has never seemed natural for man to feature in this solitude."[2]

While the figure, particularly after Varley, played an increasingly important role, landscape remained the dominant motif in the province's art. Yet such dominance sometimes had about it an air of romantic unreality. Though the Vancouver Art Gallery was occupied by the single unemployed in 1938, the social reality of the depression was rarely depicted. "British Columbia at Work" was a feature exhibition of the war years, but Weston, teaching uprooted Japanese children in the internment camps at New Denver in 1944, painted only the Slocan Mountains.

In 1940 Jack Shadbolt wrote of the ease with which artists "accept our giant landscape."[3] By the 1940s British Columbians and their artists had accepted the land. Wilderness or cultivated, the landscape had become part of them. No longer exotic or alien, it was here and it was home. The conifer retained its dark solemnity, but was no longer gloomy. The coastal waters retained their awesomeness, but were no longer fearsome or foreign. The artists reflected and advanced this acceptance of the province's landscape. Their perception was sometimes lyrical and moody, sometimes abstracted, sometimes analytic, often quiet. But passionate or serene, by the end of the war the landscape of British Columbia had become natural to its inhabitants.

Once discovered, there was no longer any need to penetrate, feel or spiritualize the landscape. The spiritual unity with nature had reached its apotheosis in the works of Varley and Carr. When abstractionism was introduced from New York, British Columbia's artists quickly adopted it, moving back into city studios during the 1950s and 1960s. Although the liberation of art was also a negation of landscape, ecological awareness bred not only parodies, but a renewed concern for the land. Profiles, silhouettes, and suggestive colour and light emerged from the hard-edged canvases of Gordon Smith and the swirling collages of Toni Onley. Art was again reflecting the perceptions of an age now ill at ease in the environment it had made home.

Notes

PREFACE

1 Roy Daniells, "National Identity in English-Canadian Writing," in K.L. Goodwin, ed., *National Identity* (London: Heinemann Educational Books, 1970), p. 85.

2 Kenneth Clarke, *Landscape into Art* (London: John Murray, 1949), p. 47.

CHAPTER ONE   EARLY VIEWS

1 The conceptualizations for this chapter are based upon discussions by Marjorie Hope Nicolson, *Mountain Gloom and Mountain Glory* (New York: W.W. Norton, 1959); Christopher Hussey, *The Picturesque* (London: Putnam, 1927); Samuel H. Monk, *The Sublime* (Ann Arbor: University of Michigan, 1960); Elizabeth Wheeler Manwaring, *Italian Landscape in Eighteenth Century England* (New York: Oxford, 1925); and Walter John Hipple, Jr., *The Beautiful, the Sublime, and the Picturesque in Eighteenth-Century British Aesthetic Theory* (Carbondale: Southern Illinois University Press, 1957). For a larger discussion of these ideas among the explorers, see the authors' "Pleasant Diversity and Sublime Desolation: The 18th Century British Perception of the Northwest Coast," *Pacific Northwest Quarterly,* Vol. LXV (January, 1974), pp. 1-7.

2 Captain George Vancouver, *Voyage of Discovery to the North Pacific Ocean, and Round the World* 3 vols. (London: G.G. and J. Robinson and J. Edwards, 1798), Vol. I, p. 200.

3 *Ibid.,* Vol. I, pp. 227-8.

4 *Ibid.,* Vol. I, pp. 226, 259.

5 *Ibid.,* Vol. I, p. 321.

6 John Meares, *Voyages Made in the Years 1788 and 1789* (London: Logographic Press, 1790), p. 233.

7 Captain George Dixon, *Voyage Round the World* (London: Geo. Goulding, 1789), p. 246.

8 Vancouver, *Voyage,* Vol. I, p. 321.

9 C.F. Newcombe, ed., *Menzies' Journal of Vancouver's Voyage, April to October, 1792,* Archives of British Columbia Memoir No. V (Victoria: British Columbia Archives, 1923), pp. 62, 76, 112.

10 James Cook, *Voyage to the Pacific Ocean* (London: Lords Commissioners of the Admiralty by W. and A. Strachan, G. Nicol and T. Cadell, 1784), Vol. I, p. 5.

11 Adm. 2/735, Admiralty Secretary to Webber, June 24, 1776, in J.C. Beaglehole, ed., *The Journals of Captain James Cook on His Voyage of Discovery,* Vol. III: *The Voyage of the Resolution and Discovery, 1776-1780* (Cambridge: The University Press for the Hakluyt Society, 1967), Part II, p. 1507.

12 Bernard Smith, *European Vision and the South Pacific* (Oxford: Clarendon Press, 1960), p. 77.

13 Beaglehole, ed., *Journals of Cook,* Vol. III, Part I, p. 306.

14 Samwell to Gregson, May 16, 1784, in *ibid.,* Vol. III, Part II, p. lxxxvi.

15 Vancouver, *Voyage,* Vol. I, p. xiv.

16 Quoted in Donald C. Cutter, "Early Spanish Artists on the Northwest Coast," *Pacific Northwest Quarterly*, Vol. LIV (October, 1963), pp. 150-7.

17 Newcombe, ed., *Menzies' Journal*, p. 128.

18 William Gilpin, *Remarks on Forest Scenery, and Other Woodland Views*, ed. Sir Thomas Dick Lauder, orig. 1791 (Edinburgh: Fraser, 1834), Vol. I, p. 174.

19 "Account of the Voyage Made by the Schooner 'Sutil' & 'Mexicana' in the Year 1792 to Survey the Strait of Fuca," typescript in British Columbia Archives, translated by G.F. Barwick from the Spanish publication of 1802, pp. 68-9. The archive version is attributed to José Espinosa y Tello, although it was probably written by Cardero.

20 Alexander Mackenzie, *Voyages from Montreal* (London: Cadell, Jun. and W. Davies, 1801), p. 378.

21 J.B. Tyrell, ed., *David Thompson's Narrative of His Explorations in Western America, 1784-1812* (Toronto: The Champlain Society, 1916), p. 554. Three of the sketches are reproduced as endpapers to this volume.

22 W. Kaye Lamb, ed., *The Letters and Journals of Simon Fraser, 1806-1808* (Toronto: Macmillan, 1960), pp. 63, 73, 76-7.

CHAPTER TWO   ILLUSTRATION AND REPORTAGE

1 James Douglas to James Hargrave, February 5, 1843, in G.P. de T. Glazebrook, ed., *The Hargrave Correspondence, 1821-1843* (Toronto: The Champlain Society, 1938), pp. 420, 421.

2 *Ibid.*, pp. 420-1.

3 Berthold Seemann, *Narrative of the Voyage of H.M.S. Herald during the Years 1845-51* (London: Reeve and Co., 1853), pp. 102, 97.

4 Charles Ross to Donald Ross, January 10, 1844, in W.K. Lamb, ed., "Five Letters of Charles Ross, 1842-44," *British Columbia Historical Quarterly*, Vol. VII (April, 1943), p. 111.

5 W. Colquohoun Grant, "Description of Vancouver Island," *Journal of the Royal Geographical Society*, Vol. XXVI (1852), p. 272; J. Despard Pemberton, *Facts and Figures Relating to Vancouver Island and British Columbia* (London: Longman, Green, Longman, and Roberts, 1860), p. 9.

6 Grant, *Journal of Geographical Society*, Vol. XXVI, p. 269.

7 Commander R.C. Mayne, *Four Years in British Columbia and Vancouver Island* (London: John Murray, 1862), p. 43.

8 Grant, *Journal of Geographical Society*, Vol. XXVI, p. 272.

9 Public Archives of Canada, Henry J. Warre Papers, "Willamette Vally, Oregon, Sept. 1845," p. 27; "Private Journal & Notes on the Oregon Territory During a Winter's Residence to the End of 1845," p. 1241.

10 Grant, *Journal of Geographical Society*, Vol. XXVI, p. 311.

11 Warre Papers, "Private Journal," p. 1237.

12 *Ibid.*, "Return Journey across the Rocky Mountains from Fort Vancouver—Columbia to Fort Garry on Red River," pp. 2082-3.

13 *Ibid.*, p. 2084.

14 Paul Kane, *Wanderings of an Artist*, in J. Russell Harper, *Paul Kane's Frontier* (Austin: University of Texas Press, 1971), p. 121.

[15] *British Columbia and Vancouver Island* (Durham: Wm. Ainsley, 1865), pp. 36-7.

[16] Capt. C.E. Barrett-Lennard, *Travels in British Columbia* (London: Hurst and Blackett, 1862), pp. 142-3.

[17] Mayne, *Four Years,* p. 105.

[18] *Prize Essay and Poem of the Literary Institute, Victoria, V. I.* (Victoria: J.E. McMillan, 1868).

[19] *Ibid.,* pp. 4, 5, 11.

[20] *Ibid.,* p. 13.

[21] *Harper's New Monthly Magazine,* Vol. XXXIX (November, 1869), pp. 793-817.

[22] J. Russell Harper, *William G.R. Hind (1833-1888)* (Windsor, Ont.: Willistead Art Gallery, 1967), n.p.

[23] *The British Colonist* (Victoria), March 12, 1863, p. 3.

[24] British Columbia Archives, Vancouver Island Exploratory Expedition Papers, Correspondence Inward, Coleman to VIEE, May 11, 1864; May 23, 1864.

[25] *Ibid.,* Richardson to VIEE, May 18, 1864.

[26] *Ibid.,* Whymper to VIEE, May 10, 1864; Whymper to Brown, May 23, 1864.

[27] Frederick Whymper, *Travel and Adventure in the Territory of Alaska* (London: John Murray, 1868), p. 15.

[28] *The British Colonist,* December 1, 1863, p. 3.

[29] *Ibid.,* March 17, 1864, p. 3.

[30] *Ibid.,* May 18, 1864, p. 3.

[31] Whymper, *Travel and Adventure,* p. 44.

CHAPTER THREE   PURSUING THE EXOTIC

[1] Thomas Mower Martin, "An Artist's Letter from the Rockies," *The Week* (Toronto), October 4, 1889, p. 700.

[2] Lucius O'Brien, "Grandeur of the Rockies," *The British Colonist* (Victoria), September 11, 1887, p. 3.

[3] J.A. Fraser, "An Artist's Experience in the Canadian Rockies," in G.M. Fairchild, Jr., ed., *Canadian Leaves* (New York: Napoléon Thompson, 1887), pp. 242, 244.

[4] F.M. Bell-Smith, "An Artist's Reminiscences," *Canadian Alpine Journal,* Vol. IX (1918), pp. 90-7.

[5] Mower Martin, *The Week* (Toronto), August 30, 1889, p. 617; September 18, 1889, pp. 648-9; September 27, 1889, p. 682; October 4, 1889, pp. 699-700.

[6] *Ibid.,* November 22, 1895, p. 1241.

[7] *Ibid.*

[8] Fraser in Fairchild, ed., *Canadian Leaves,* p. 239.

[9] *Ibid.,* pp. 234-5.

[10] O'Brien, *The British Colonist* (Victoria), September 11, 1887, p. 3.

[11] William Withrow, *Our Own Country* (Toronto: William Briggs, 1889), p. 524.

[12] *Ibid.,* p. 527.

[13] O'Brien, "An Artist's View," *Vancouver News-Advertiser,* January 1, 1889, p. 8.

[14] *Ibid.*

[15] John E. Staley, "The Premier Painter of the Rockies," *Maclean's Magazine,* Vol. XXV (December, 1912), p. 88.

16 Paul Duval, *Canadian Water Colours (Toronto: Burns and MacEachern, 1954),* n.p.

17 *The Evening Telegram* (Toronto), July 22, 1927, p. 14.

18 *The Week* (Toronto), December 15, 1893, p. 64.

19 *Ibid.,* September 18, 1899, p. 649.

20 British Columbia Archives, Mower Martin to Mrs. Horace P. Newman, February 21, 1914 (copy).

21 Edward Roper, *By Track and Trail through Canada* (London: W.H. Allen, 1891), n.p.

22 British Columbia Archives, Papers relating to C.A. de L'Aubinière, de L'Aubinière to Robson, March 6, 1887.

23 *The British Colonist* (Victoria), June 24, 1887, p. 4.

24 Emily Carr, *Growing Pains* (Toronto: Clarke Irwin, 1971; original ed., 1946), p. 76.

CHAPTER FOUR   MAINTAINING A TRADITION, 1900-25

1 "The Alpine Club of Canada," *Alpine Club of Canada,* Vol. I (1907), p. 3; H. Glynn Ward, *The Glamour of British Columbia* (New York: The Century Co., 1926), p. 164.

2 Frances Macnas, *British Columbia for Settlers* (London: Champion and Hall, 1898), p. 157.

3 Rudyard Kipling, *Letters of Travel, 1892-1913* (London: Macmillan, 1920), pp. 188, 187.

4 Rupert Brooke, *Letters from America* (Toronto: McClelland, Goodchild and Stewart, 1926), pp. 150-4.

5 *The Victoria Daily Colonist,* December 13, 1908, Section II, p. 1.

6 British Columbia Archives, Island Arts and Crafts Society Papers, J. Rutherford Blaikie, "Designing Pictures and Ideas of Beauty," published lecture to the Island Arts and Crafts Society, 1913-14.

7 Emily Carr, *Growing Pains* (Toronto: Clarke Irwin, 1971; original ed., 1946), p. 157.

8 James Leyland, "Art in Photography," *Western Women's Weekly,* Vol. I (April 18, 1918), p. 2.

9 British Columbia Archives, Josephine Crease Papers, Josephine Crease to Lady Crease, n.d. [1918].

10 Macnas, *British Columbia for Settlers,* p. 188.

11 John Kyle, "Sketching from Nature," *Westward Ho!,* Vol. III (September, 1908), p. 153.

12 *Ibid.,* Vol. III (August, 1908), p. 54.

13 John Borradaile, *Lady of Culzean* (Victoria: Beaver Books, 1971), n.p.

14 James Leyland, "Pictures: Their Choice and Decorative Value," *Western Women's Weekly,* Vol. I (February 14, 1918), p. 2.

15 *The Victoria Daily Times,* September 28, 1910, p. 7.

16 *The British Colonist* (Victoria), July 18, 1888, p. 4; R.R. MacKay Fripp, "The Island Arts Club," *The Victoria Daily Colonist,* October 8, 1911, p. 12.

17 *The Victoria Daily Colonist,* August 25, 1929, p. 10.

18 Quoted from a London newspaper in *ibid.,* June 4, 1909, p. 8.

[19] *The Daily News-Advertiser* (Vancouver), October 16, 1904, p. 5; *The Province* (Vancouver), October 16, 1904, p. 7.

[20] *The Province* (Vancouver), June 5, 1920, p. 3.

[21] "Mr. Thomas W. Fripp," Vancouver Art, Scientific and Historical Society, *Museum Notes,* No. 2 (February, 1927), p. 12.

[22] British Columbia Archives, Blaikie lecture.

[23] H. Stuart Thompson, *George A. Fripp and Alfred D. Fripp* (London: Walker's Quarterly, 1927), p. 30.

[24] "Fripp," *Museum Notes,* No. 2 (February, 1927), p. 12.

[25] *Ibid.*

[26] Walter J. Phillips, "Art and Artists," *Winnipeg Tribune,* n.d., clipping in National Gallery of Canada, Artist File, June, 1931.

[27] *The Province* (Vancouver), June 26, 1909, p. 3.

[28] C.F.J. Galloway, *The Call of the West* (London: T. Fisher Unwin, n.d.), p. 249.

[29] *The Province* (Vancouver), August 22, 1922, p. 3.

[30] "Pogue," *Western Women's Weekly,* Vol. II (October 4, 1919), p. 4.

[31] J. Butterfield, "Pictures at B.C. Fine Arts," *The Province* (Vancouver), September 19, 1921, p. 12.

CHAPTER FIVE   DIVERGENCES

[1] J. Butterfield, "B.C. Fine Arts Society Exhibition," *The Province* (Vancouver), May 19, 1923, p. 6.

[2] *The Observer* (London), quoted in Luscombe Carroll, *The Art of Charles John Collings* (London: The Carroll Gallery, 1912), p. 10.

[3] Carroll, *Collings,* p. 4.

[4] Walter J. Phillips, "Art and Artists," *Winnipeg Tribune,* August 15, 1931, in National Gallery of Canada, Artist File.

[5] *The Queen* (London), quoted in Carroll, *Collings,* p. 10.

[6] Phillips, *Winnipeg Tribune,* August 15, 1931.

[7] P.D. Konody, "Charles John Collings," *Apollo,* Vol. I (June, 1925), p. 349.

[8] Victor Reinaecker, *Charles John Collings* (privately published, n.d.), p. 21.

[9] Konody, *Apollo,* Vol. I (June, 1925), p. 349.

[10] Emily Carr, *Growing Pains* (Toronto: Clarke Irwin, 1971; original ed., 1946), p. 157.

[11] Interview with Mr. Guy Collings, August, 1973; August, 1974.

[12] Konody, *Apollo,* Vol. 1 (June, 1925), p. 349.

[13] Phillips, "Wet Paint," unpublished typescript in possession of Mr. John C. Crabb, Winnipeg, p. 45.

[14] *Ibid.,* p. 106.

[15] *Ibid.,* p. 14.

[16] Phillips, "Art and Artists," *Winnipeg Evening Tribune,* August 3, 1946.

[17] Phillips, "Pictures on the Wall," unpublished typescript in possession of Mr. John C. Crabb, Winnipeg, n.p.

[18] Phillips, *An Essay in Wood-Cuts* (Toronto: Thomas Nelson & Sons, 1930), n.p.

[19] "Diogenes" [Bernard McEvoy], "B.C. Society of Fine Arts," *The Province* (Vancouver), April 28, 1928, p. 6.

[20] Robert Henri to Statira Frame, February 19, 1918, in possession of Mrs. Molly Underhill.

[21] Isabel True, "Armin Hansen," unpublished typescript in the library of the Monterey Peninsula Museum of Art Association, n.p.

[22] Emily Carr to Molly Frame, quoted in Eileen Johnson, "Sunlight from a Forgotten Attic," *Vancouver Life,* July, 1967, p. 19.

[23] "A Local Woman Artist," *Western Women's Weekly,* Vol. I (October 5, 1918), p. 7.

[24] Carr, *Growing Pains,* pp. 227-40.

[25] *The Vancouver Sun,* May 1, 1928, p. 5.

[26] J. Butterfield, "Fine Arts Exhibition," *The Province* (Vancouver), September 19, 1922, p. 6.

[27] *Ibid.,* September 16, 1918, p. 4.

[28] *The Province* (Vancouver), May 11, 1925, p. 12; *The Vancouver Sun,* May 1, 1928, p. 5.

[29] *The Province* (Vancouver), October 1, 1919, p. 16.

CHAPTER SIX   THE EROSION OF ISOLATION

[1] J.E.H. MacDonald, "A Glimpse of the West," *Canadian Bookman,* Vol. VI (November, 1924), pp. 229-31.

[2] Barker Fairley, "The Group of Seven," *Canadian Forum,* Vol. V (February, 1925), p. 146.

[3] A.Y. Jackson, "Recollections on My Seventieth Birthday," *Canadian Art,* Vol. X (Spring, 1953), p. 99.

[4] F.B. Housser, "Some Thoughts on National Consciousness," *Canadian Theosophist,* Vol. VIII (July 15, 1927), p. 82.

[5] J.E.H. MacDonald, *New Statesman,* 1919, quoted in F.B. Housser, *A Canadian Art Movement* (Toronto: Macmillan of Canada, 1926), p. 143; Arthur Lismer, "Canadian Art," *Canadian Theosophist,* Vol. V (February 15, 1925), p. 179.

[6] Lismer, *Canadian Theosophist,* Vol. V (February 15, 1925), p. 179.

[7] Lismer, quoted in John A.R. McLeish, *September Gale* (Toronto: J.M. Dent & Sons, 1955), p. 186.

[8] Lawren Harris, quoted in Bess Harris and R.G.P. Colgrove, eds., *Lawren Harris* (Toronto: Macmillan of Canada, 1969), p. 14; Lismer, *Canadian Theosophist,* Vol. V (February 15, 1925), p. 178.

[9] Phillips, "Art and Artists," undated clipping from the *Winnipeg Evening Tribune,* in possession of Mr. John C. Crabb, Winnipeg.

[10] See Roderick Nash, *Wilderness and the American Mind* (New Haven: Yale University Press, 1967); Peter J. Schmitt, *Back to Nature* (New York: Oxford University Press, 1968).

[11] For an excellent treatment of the ideas and intellectual sources of the Group, see Mary Vipond, "National Consciousness in English-Speaking Canada in the 1920s: Seven Studies," unpublished Ph.D. thesis, University of Toronto, 1974.

[12] Ruth D. Golman, "Garibaldi Park," *Canadian Geographical Journal,* No. 3 (November, 1931), p. 339.

[13] Garibaldi Park Board, *Garibaldi Park* (Victoria: B.C. Department of Lands, 1929), p. 3.

[14] A.H. Sovereign, "Garibaldi Park," *British Columbia Monthly,* No. 23 (October-November, 1921), p. 9.

CHAPTER SEVEN   THE FIRST CONSCIOUS EXPRESSION OF THE RHYTHM OF LIFE

[1] National Gallery of Canada, J.W.G. Macdonald to Harry McCurry, October 24, 1938.

[2] Emily Carr, *The Book of Small* (Toronto: Clarke Irwin, 1966; original edition, 1942), pp. 70, 8, 84, 85.

[3] Emily Carr, illustrated journal of a bicycle trip to Cowichan, B.C., 1895. Private Collection.

[4] Emily Carr, *Growing Pains* (Toronto: Clarke Irwin, 1971; original edition, 1946), pp. 80, 78, 79.

[5] A.G. Folliott Stokes, "The Landscape Paintings of Mr. Algernon M. Talmage," *International Studio,* Vol. XXXIII (January, 1908), p. 188.

[6] Carr, *Growing Pains*, p. 181.

[7] Arnold Watson, "In the Haunts of a Picture Maker" *The Week,* February 18, 1905, pp. 1, 2; Carr, *Growing Pains,* p. 185.

[8] Carr, *Growing Pains,* p. 207.

[9] *Ibid.,* p. 227.

[10] Viola Patterson to Maria Tippett, October 5, 1973, in possession of the authors.

[11] Jan Gordon, *Modern French Painters* (London: John Lane, The Bodley Head, 1923), p. 31.

[12] Emily Carr, *Hundreds and Thousands* (Toronto: Clarke Irwin, 1966), p. 5.

[13] *Ibid.,* p. 7.

[14] *Ibid.,* p. 21.

[15] Carr, *Growing Pains,* p. 238.

[16] *Ibid.,* p. 254.

[17] Carr, *Hundreds and Thousands,* p. 66.

[18] *Ibid.,* pp. 207, 146.

[19] *Ibid.,* p. 57.

[20] *Ibid.,* p. 132.

[21] *Ibid.,* p. 29.

[22] *Ibid.,* pp. 35, 64, 46, 48.

[23] University of British Columbia Library, Special Collections, Nan Lawson Cheney Papers, Carr to Cheney, February 13, 1941.

[24] Carr, *Hundreds and Thousands,* p. 148.

[25] *Ibid.,* p. 5.

[26] National Gallery of Canada, J.W.G. Macdonald to Harry McCurry, October 24, 1938.

CHAPTER EIGHT   SEARCH FOR FORM AND ESSENCE

[1] Grace Melvin, "Pattern," Vancouver School of Decorative and Applied Art, *The Paint Box,* Vol. III (June, 1928), pp. 51, 50.

[2] *The Province* (Vancouver), November 9, 1935, p. 7.

[3] Arthur Lismer, "F.H. Varley: The Early Years," in Art Gallery of Toronto, *F.H. Varley* (Toronto: Art Gallery of Toronto, 1954), p. 4.

[4] National Gallery of Canada [hereafter NGC], Varley to Dr. J.M. MacCallum, n.d., quoted in Peter Mellon, *The Group of Seven* (Toronto: McClelland and Stewart, 1970), p. 41.

[5] Arthur Lismer, "F.H. Varley: The Twenties," in Art Gallery of Toronto, *Varley,* p. 7.

[6] NGC Varley to Eric Brown, August 10, 1926.

[7] *The Province* (Vancouver), September 19, 1926, p. 13.

[8] *Ibid.*

[9] NGC, taped interview with Miss Beatrice Lennie by Ann Pollock, 1969.

[10] J.W.G. Macdonald, "F.H. Varley, Vancouver," in Art Gallery of Toronto, *Varley*, pp. 7, 8.

[11] Quoted in Donald W. Buchanan, "The Paintings and Drawings of F.H. Varley," *Canadian Art*, Vol. VII (Autumn, 1949), p. 3.

[12] Varley, untitled, *The Paint Box*, Vol. III (June, 1928), p. 12.

[13] Varley, "Room 27 Speaking," in *ibid.*, Vol. II (June, 1927), p. 23.

[14] McKenzie Porter, "Varley," *Maclean's Magazine*, Vol. LXXII (November 7, 1959), p. 63.

[15] NGC, Varley to Eric Brown, December 7, 1935.

[16] *Ibid.*, February 1, [1936].

[17] *Ibid.*, December 26, 1935.

[18] Interview with Miss Beatrice Lennie by Ann Wood, 1973, quoted in Ann Wood, unpublished typescript in possession of authors.

[19] Macdonald, "The Ever Open Book in the Matter of Design," *The Paint Box*, Vol. II (June, 1927), p. 47.

[20] Burnaby Art Gallery, Macdonald to G.H. Tyler, January 2, 1936 (copy).

[21] *Ibid.*

[22] Burnaby Art Gallery, Macdonald to John Varley, December 8, 1937 [*sic*, 1936], (copy); Macdonald to G.H. Tyler, January 2, 1936, (copy).

[23] Maxwell Bates, "Jock Macdonald, Painter-Explorer," *Canadian Art*, Vol. XIV (Summer, 1957), p. 152.

[24] NGC, Macdonald to Harry McCurry, March 26, 1937.

[25] *Ibid.*, October 23, 1937.

[26] *Ibid.*, Macdonald to Eric Brown, September 7, 1938; Macdonald to Harry McCurry, September 7, 1938.

[27] *Ibid.*, Macdonald to Nan Lawson Cheney, July 20, 1939, (copy), June 27, 1947 (copy).

[28] Glenbow-Alberta Institute, taped interview with Mr. W.P. Weston by Margery Dalles, 1962.

[29] "Diogenes" [Bernard McEvoy], "The B.C. Society of Fine Art," *The Province* (Vancouver), June 10, 1930, p. 6.

[30] Mac Reynolds, "Cabbage—It Can be Art," *The Vancouver Sun*, April 24, 1959, p. 3.

[31] Glenbow-Alberta Institute, taped interview with W.P. Weston.

[32] *Ibid.*

[33] *Ibid.*

[34] Undated manuscript in possession of Mrs. Doris Woods, n.p.

[35] Glenbow-Alberta Institute, taped interview with W.P. Weston.

[36] Undated manuscript, Mrs. Woods, n.p.

[37] Glenbow-Alberta Institute, taped interview with W.P. Weston.

[38] *Ibid.*

[39] Thomas Hart Benton, quoted in Matthew Baigell, ed., *A Thomas Hart Benton Miscellany* (Lawrence: University Press of Kansas, 1971), p. 3.

[40] Graham Collier, *Form, Space, and Vision* (Englewood Cliffs, N.J.: Prentice Hall, 1963), p. 30.

[41] Glenbow-Alberta Institute, taped interview with W.P. Weston.

CHAPTER NINE   AN END—OR A BEGINNING?

[1] Vito Cianci, "Artists—And Others," Vancouver School of Decorative and Applied Art, *The Paint Box*, Vol. III (June, 1928), pp. 14-15.

[2] Quoted in Bob Allen, "New Picture of Shadbolt Takes Form," *The Province* (Vancouver), November 21, 1973, p. 15.

[3] *Ibid.*

[4] University of British Columbia Library, Special Collections, Nan Lawson Cheney Papers, Carr to Nan Lawson Cheney, May 10, 1942.

[5] Allen, *The Province*, November 21, 1973, p. 15.

[6] Authors' interview with Mr. J.L. Shadbolt, July, 1973.

[7] Shadbolt, *In Search of Form* (Toronto: McClelland and Stewart, 1968), p. 64.

[8] Uhthoff memoirs, p. 3, typescript, private collection.

[9] *Ibid.*, pp. 9-10.

[10] National Gallery of Canada, taped interview with Rowina Morrell by Ann Pollock, 1969.

[11] Alice Macpherson, "Climbing," *The Paint Box*, Vol. V (December, 1930), p. 11.

[12] Earle Birney, "David," in *David* (Toronto: Ryerson, 1942), p. 1; "Waterton Holiday," in *ibid.*, p. 12. Reprinted by permission of McClelland and Stewart, Ltd., Toronto.

[13] Cianci, "Morning on the Black Tusk Meadows," *The Paint Box*, Vol. III (June, 1928), p. 63.

[14] Shadbolt, *In Search of Form*, p. 64-5.

[15] Birney, "Hands," in *Now is Time* (Toronto: Ryerson, 1945), p. 13; "Dusk on the Bay," in *ibid.*, p. 17. Reprinted by permission of McClelland and Stewart, Ltd., Toronto.

[16] National Gallery of Canada, J.W.G. Macdonald to Harry McCurry, December 2, 1939.

[17] *Ibid.*, May 10, 1943.

[18] University of British Columbia Library, Cheney Papers, Carr to Cheney, February 26, 1941; May 30, 1941.

[19] Birney, "'And the Earth Grew Young Again,'" in *Now is Time*, p. 34. Reprinted by permission of McClelland and Stewart, Ltd., Toronto.

[20] "Palette" [J. Delisle Parker], "At the Art Gallery," *The Province* (Vancouver), May 16, 1942, p. 16.

[21] Browni Wingate, "Annual Exhibition of Fine Arts Provides Interesting Display," *The Vancouver News-Herald*, May 16, 1944, p. 13.

[22] "Palette" [J. Delisle Parker], "In the Realm of Art," *The Province* (Vancouver), May 21, 1943, p. 6; Mildred Valley Thornton, "'No-Jury' B.C. Show Triumph for Artists," *The Vancouver Sun*, September 27, 1943, p. 11.

[23] Quoted in Donald W. Buchanan, "Shadbolt Explores a World of Roots and Seeds," *Canadian Art*, No. 9 (Spring, 1951), p. 114.

[24] Alvin Balkind, *Beyond Regionalism*, quoted in Doreen Walker, "The Treatment

of Nature in Canadian Art since the Group of Seven," M.A., University of British Columbia, 1969, p. 157.

25 Doris Shadbolt, "B.C.'s *New Talent* Show to Tour Canada," *Canadian Art,* No. 21 (September-October, 1964), p. 301.

26 Walker, "Treatment of Nature," Ch. VIII.

27 Baxter, *Statements: 18 Canadian Artists,* p. 14, quoted in *ibid.,* p. 207.

28 Gene Youngblood, "World Game: The Artists as Ecologist," *Artscanada* (August, 1970), p. 46.

29 Thomas Garver, "British Columbia: 'I've Got to Get Backed Up against the Bush,'" *Artscanada* (December, 1969), pp. 31, 32.

30 Joan Lowndes, "Gordon Smith: A New Perspective," *Artscanada* (August, 1973), p. 60.

EPILOGUE

1 Eric Nicol, *Vancouver* (Toronto: Doubleday Canada, 1970), p. 127.

2 Reta W. Myers, "In the Domain of Art," *The Province* (Vancouver), October 9, 1932, p. 7; Weston, undated manuscript in the possession of Mrs. Doris Woods; Shadbolt, "Epilogue," Vancouver School of Art, *Behind the Palette,* 1939-40, n.p.

3 "Epilogue," *Behind the Palette,* 1939-40, n.p.

A NOTE ON SOURCES

For those interested in further study, the notes which accompany the text will prove useful. An article "Art in British Columbia—The Historical Sources," which appeared in *B.C. Studies,* No. 23, Fall, 1974, covers most of the sources known to the authors. In addition to that survey several recent books might be mentioned. Michael Bell, *Painters in a New Land* (Toronto: McClelland and Stewart, 1973) and Lorne Render, *The Mountains and the Sky* (Calgary: Glenbow/McClelland and Stewart West, 1974) are useful for their illustrations of pictures in the Public Archives of Canada and the Glenbow-Alberta Institute respectively. A short but fine chapter dealing with Varley, Macdonald and Carr is contained in Charles C. Hill, *Canadian Painting in the Thirties* (Ottawa: The National Gallery of Canada, 1975). J. Russell Harper has added to our knowledge of Hind in his monograph, *W.G.R. Hind* (Ottawa: National Museums, 1976).

Photo Credits

British Library Board: 20
Dominion Gallery, Montreal: 131 (bottom)
Tod Greenaway, Vancouver: 44, 45, 56 (bottom), 64, 65, 67, 69, 73,
     76, 77, 80 (top), 81, 95 (top left), 100, 104, 107, 111, 114,
     115 (top), 123, 126 (left), 126 (bottom right), 127
Hans Jorgensen, Seattle: 96
Ken McAllister, Vancouver: 99 (right), 119
The McMichael Canadian Collection, Kleinburg, Ontario: 87, 89,
     102, 109
Montreal Museum of Fine Art: 88
National Gallery of Canada, Ottawa: 39, 52, 54, 115 (bottom),
     131 (top)
National Library of Australia, Canberra: 19 (bottom), 21
National Maritime Museum, London, England: 19 (top)
Toni Onley: 134
Simon Fraser University, Audio Visual Department: 56 (top right),
     61, 80 (bottom), 126 (top right)
George Tiessen: 138
University of British Columbia: 23
Vancouver Art Gallery: 68, 95 (bottom), 101, 132, 133, 135
Lynn Vardaman, Vancouver: 116

Index